Tom Cruise's True North

The Unfiltered Story of Hollywood's Maverick Secret. Navigating Fame, Faith, and Family

Adam Newton

TABLE OF CONTENT

CHAPTER 7

EVOLUTION OF STYLE. 48

CHAPTER 8

FILMOGRAPHY ANALYSIS. 53

INTRODUCTION

In the arena of stars and silver screens, there exists a man whose career defies convention, whose presence ignites the celluloid, and whose name endures beyond generations: Tom Cruise. This book begins on an intensive journey into the life, career, and mysterious allure of a Hollywood legend who has left an everlasting stamp on the cinematic world.

Beyond the incessant flashbulbs and the shallow plots, Tom Cruise stands as a paragon of cinematic talent and devotion. This is not only a history of fame, but a tribute to a magnificent voyage that began modestly and built its road to the heights of superstardom. From the humble roots of a passionate young actor to the dominating presence he is now, every tale unravels the layers of devotion and tenacity that have molded his journey.

This story unearths the events that occurred behind the scenes - tales of teamwork, artistic zeal, and the unrelenting quest for excellence. Collaborations with great filmmakers, co-stars who became confidants, and the sweat and emotion spent into making those iconic cinematic moments are the threads weaved across these pages. Delve into the trials that tested his mettle and the successes that reinforced his standing as a cinematic powerhouse.

Yet, Tom Cruise is more than simply an actor. He is an embodiment of influence, a builder of trends, and a prism through which to examine the ever-shifting dynamics of popular culture. His distinctive charm is not a mere characteristic; it is an aura that transcends the screen, generating trends and attitudes that echo well beyond the box office. From the origins of his success to the fan culture that supports it, this book aims to deconstruct the components that make Tom Cruise not simply a celebrity, but a lasting cultural icon.

Beyond the brilliant lights of Hollywood, the guy beneath the roles owns a personal narrative that is as intriguing as any script. Marriages and romances, the balancing act of celebrity and family, and the humanitarian initiatives that define his character are parts of his life that this book uncovers with an honest gaze. Moreover, the complex interplay of religion, beliefs, and the choices he has made gives a window into the delicate mosaic of his personality.

As we journey further, we examine the adrenaline-fueled core of Tom Cruise's career - the audacious feats and magnificent action scenes that have pushed the frontiers of cinematic daring. This inquiry dissects the calculated risks, the physical and mental challenges, and the transformational influence these accomplishments have on his body of work and his reputation as an unrivaled action hero.

Tom Cruise's reputation is interlaced with moments of controversy that fueled intense arguments. Yet, he stands as a phoenix that rises from the ashes, time and again, forging comebacks that reinvent his story. From negotiating media hazards to recovering his stature, these moments provide a tribute to his tenacity and his uncompromising determination.

Buckle up as we start on this thrilling excursion inside the intriguing realm of Tom Cruise. This is not simply a biography; it is an investigation of the man, the artist, and the phenomena that continue to impact the world of cinema and culture. Prepare to be intrigued, informed, and absorbed in the incredible narrative of Tom Cruise, the legend who has permanently engraved his name in the annals of entertainment history.

CHAPTER 1

BIOGRAPHY AND CAREER EVOLUTION

Early Life and Introduction to Acting

Tom Cruise's path into the world of acting began in the heart of Syracuse, New York. Born on July 3, 1962, as Thomas Cruise Mapother IV, he demonstrated a passion for performance from an early age. Raised in a household characterized by continual migration, Cruise's youth was affected by his parent's divorce and the following relocations.

Amidst these hurdles, his interest in acting burgeoned. At age 14, Cruise watched a school show that kindled his enthusiasm. Fuelled by a drive to escape his terrible surroundings, he embraced acting with enthusiasm. This passion led him to the Lee Strasberg Theatre Institute, where he developed his technique.

Breakthrough Roles and Rise to Stardom

Cruise's climb from aspiring actor to Hollywood celebrity was propelled by a series of critical breakthroughs. His debut film appearance occurred in 1981 with "Endless Love," delivering a peek at his raw potential. However, it was "Risky Business" (1983) that pushed him to the mainstream. Portraying a dynamic high schooler, Cruise exhibited a distinct combination of charm and energy that connected with moviegoers.

This achievement cleared the way for his performance in "Top Gun" (1986), establishing his career as a leading man. The film's high-flying action and Cruise's magnetic personality captured spectators, turning him into a household brand. His reputation as a conscientious performer increased, and he welcomed tough assignments that displayed his range.

Iconic Roles and Continual Success

Cruise's career trajectory hit new heights with a succession of classic performances that demonstrated his depth and flexibility. "Rain Man" (1988) spotlighted his ability to tackle difficult characters, gaining him critical praise. The 1990s saw him reinvent action filmmaking with the "Mission: Impossible" franchise, where his drive to undertake risky exploits enthralled worldwide audiences.

Continual achievement comes not just via action but also through drama. In "Jerry Maguire" (1996), Cruise's role as a sports agent battling with ethics showcased his emotional versatility. His partnership with innovative directors, such as Stanley Kubrick in "Eyes Wide Shut" (1999), reinforced his image as an actor unafraid to explore new genres.

Cruise's career is one of transformation, from a driven adolescent with a goal to an international celebrity known for his commitment to his profession. His early life challenges and undying passion for performing have established his status as an enduring legend in the world of cinema.

CHAPTER 2

BEHIND-THE-SCENES INSIGHTS

Collaborations with Directors and Co-Stars

Tom Cruise's career in Hollywood is distinguished not only by his legendary parts but also by his exceptional partnerships with innovative filmmakers and skilled co-stars. From his early career to the current day, Cruise has demonstrated a unique ability to choose films that not only challenge his acting talents but also allow him to work alongside some of the industry's sharpest brains. His cooperation with filmmaker Steven Spielberg, for instance, resulted in cinematic classics like "Minority Report" and "War of the Worlds." Their cooperation brought out Cruise's flexibility and Spielberg's aptitude for constructing fascinating storylines.

Another notable cooperation was with famed filmmaker Christopher McQuarrie, who oversaw many "Mission: Impossible" movies. Their creative relationship enhanced the action genre, providing a feeling of realism and a heart-pounding thrill to each picture. Co-stars like Emily Blunt in "Edge of Tomorrow" and Jamie Foxx in "Collateral" added to the chemistry that fueled these movies, making them more than just action-packed spectacles. The subtle interplay between Cruise and his colleagues frequently led to performances that connected emotionally with viewers and critics alike, displaying his capacity to inspire those around him.

Crafting Unforgettable Movie Moments

Behind every famous film, there lurks a succession of moments that stay carved in viewers' brains. Tom Cruise's career is decorated with such moments—scenes that have become part of cinematic history. Consider the exhilarating sequence in "Top Gun" where Cruise's Maverick soars to the sky, embodying a sense of freedom and exhilaration. This wasn't simply a sequence; it was a turning point that confirmed Cruise's image as a compelling leading man.

In "Jerry Maguire," Cruise's emotionally intense "You complete me" monologue to Renée Zellweger's character is a tribute to his ability to put real emotions into his performances. This sequence struck emotionally with spectators, displaying his breadth beyond action-packed parts. And who could forget the gravity-defying Burj Khalifa feat in "Mission: Impossible - Ghost Protocol"? This moment wasn't just about defying physics; it reflected the passion and bravery Cruise takes to his profession, often pushing the edges of what's possible in filmmaking.

These moments aren't accidents; they are painstakingly produced by a determined actor who not only adores the people he plays but also elevates them into cultural touchstones. Tom Cruise's passion for his parts means that each movie he's a part of contains moments that continue to resound in the hearts of viewers long after the credits roll.

Challenges and Triumphs on Set

When it comes to filming, problems often occur as an intrinsic part of the process, and Tom Cruise's filmography is no exception. Throughout his lengthy career, he has experienced a range of problems on set, each addressed with his unrelenting passion and perseverance. One such case may be discovered in the filming of "Mission: Impossible - Fallout." The daring airborne feats and dramatic action sequences needed rigorous preparation and execution. Cruise's devotion to realism dictated that he undertake several of these feats himself, resulting in tough logistics and precise coordination with the team. The victory in this case wasn't simply the magnificent spectacle portrayed on screen, but the collaborative spirit that evolved from conquering these hurdles, culminating in a film that stretched the frontiers of action filmmaking.

In the domain of historical dramas, the film "Interview with the Vampire" provided a unique set of obstacles for Tom Cruise and the team. Adapting Anne Rice's intricate work to the big screen needed great attention to detail, from historical accuracy to capturing the soul of the characters. Cruise's achievement resided in his depiction of the seductive and intriguing vampire Lestat. The problem here was not just in portraying the spirit of a character beloved by fans, but also in negotiating the complexity of the film's plot. Through his cooperation with co-stars and director Neil Jordan, Cruise managed to bring Lestat to life in a way that both appreciated the original material and highlighted his acting abilities.

In the romantic drama "Jerry Maguire," Tom Cruise had the task of playing a sports agent and experiencing a dramatic personal and professional journey. The brilliance of this picture resided in Cruise's ability to reconcile the fragility and power of his character, Jerry Maguire.

This position needed not just emotional depth but also a careful approach to relationships and personal progress. Cruise's relationship with co-star Renée Zellweger provided another element of reality to the film. Navigating these hurdles and finally producing a poignant and unforgettable performance led to the film's critical and economic success, displaying Cruise's capacity to thrive in parts beyond the action genre.

Throughout his career, Tom Cruise has experienced a variety of problems on set, each overcome with an unflinching devotion to his profession. These obstacles have not only challenged his talents but have also created possibilities for creative cooperation and progress.

As evidenced by examples such as "Mission: Impossible - Fallout," "Interview with the Vampire," and "Jerry Maguire," Cruise's triumphs over these hurdles have delivered pictures that not only entertain but also resonate on a deeper level with viewers throughout the world.

CHAPTER 3

INFLUENCE AND IMPACT

What Set Tom Cruise Apart

In the arena of Hollywood, where skill and star power clash, Tom Cruise emerges as a dazzling figure with a compelling charm that transcends simple popularity. His enigmatic attractiveness doesn't derive just from his beautiful looks and acting skills; it's a combination of numerous qualities that, when combined, produce an unforgettable impression.

Cruise's on-screen presence is laced with a tangible passion that grips fans from the time he graces the screen. He has an unusual capacity to express a gamut of emotions seamlessly, be it heart-pounding action, emotional drama, or side-splitting humor. This broad spectrum of emotional resonance renders his characters sympathetic and memorable, allowing audiences to participate fully in their cinematic journeys.

Yet, Cruise's charm isn't restricted to his acting alone. It extends to his persistent attention to his art. His determination to execute risky feats, embrace hard parts, and commit to every character he plays demonstrates a devotion that goes beyond the ordinary. This devotion develops a relationship with audiences who respect his genuineness and enthusiasm.

Moreover, his appeal is profoundly anchored in his humility and accessibility. Despite his A-list notoriety, Cruise remains down-to-earth and personable, shattering the stigma of remote superstars. This relatability promotes a sense of familiarity that supporters adore.

Shaping Hollywood Trends and Standards

Tom Cruise is more than an actor; he's an influencer who has redefined Hollywood norms and set the road for innovation. His cinematic selections and bold roles have driven genres ahead, creating new criteria for quality and inventiveness.

Cruise's involvement in revolutionary action sequences, frequently executed by him himself, has upped the expectations for action pictures. His determination to push limits and embrace risk has prompted the industry to reconsider the way stunts are conducted, upping the bar for realism and intensity.

His partnerships with imaginative directors have also developed unique narrative strategies. Movies like "Minority Report" and "Edge of Tomorrow" questioned the norms of sci-fi, while his contributions to the "Mission: Impossible" franchise rewrote the rules for action-packed spy thrillers.

Fans and Their Lasting Connection

The heart of Tom Cruise's influence and impact rests in the ongoing connection he has with his admirers. His cinematic journey has braided itself into the lives of innumerable individuals, generating a profound and lasting influence that spans decades.

Cruise's followers don't only watch his flicks; they embark on emotional odysseys alongside his characters. The feelings he elicits reverberate on a personal level, building a link that withstands the test of time. This relationship isn't restricted to a particular population; it transcends across age groups, ethnicities, and countries.

Furthermore, Cruise's relationship with his fan base displays his sincere appreciation for their constant support. From unexpected visits to fan gatherings to sincere social media exchanges, he makes his supporters feel valued and treasured. This reciprocity sustains the fan base, establishing a feeling of community that serves as a monument to his ongoing significance.

In conclusion, Tom Cruise's charm, ability to create industry trends, and intimate connection with fans all make an incredible tapestry of power. His charisma isn't simply a quality; it's a force that unifies his performances, his effect on Hollywood, and the emotions of people who have been affected by his work.

CHAPTER 4

PERSONAL LIFE AND RELATIONSHIPS

Marriages and High-Profile Romances

Tom Cruise's personal life has long been the subject of intense media scrutiny, notably his marriages and high-profile relationships. His romances have provided an insight into the problems of maintaining a private life while being one of Hollywood's most known people.

Cruise's first high-profile marriage was to actress Mimi Rogers in 1987. Their friendship brought him to Scientology, which ultimately became a crucial aspect of his life. The marriage, however, dissolved in 1990. It was his second marriage to actress Nicole Kidman in 1990 that drew great notice. The couple's on-screen chemistry transitioned to a real-life romance that enthralled the audience. Despite their supposedly deep love, their marriage came to an end in 2001.

Perhaps the most talked-about episode in Cruise's personal life was his marriage to actress Katie Holmes in 2006. Their quick courting and the public's curiosity about their interpersonal dynamics made the news globe. The media's criticism of their marriage was increased by Cruise's outspoken advocacy of Scientology and his daughter Suri's upbringing. The marriage finally dissolved in 2012.

Balancing Fame and Family

Navigating the rigors of stardom while maintaining a harmonious family life has been a tricky task for Tom Cruise. His job responsibilities regularly take him around the world for lengthy periods, necessitating careful juggling of his roles as an actor and a parent.

Cruise's loyalty to his children, Isabella and Connor, from his marriage to Nicole Kidman, has been a constant despite his demanding schedule. The problems of having a strong parental presence while being in the public glare underline the nuances of his path.

Tom Cruise's Philanthropic Endeavors

Beyond his film triumphs, Tom Cruise has also been active in several charity projects. His devotion to humanitarian activities displays a side of him that goes beyond the glitz of Hollywood.

Cruise has been a fervent supporter of groups like the Church of Scientology's activities and its connected charities, which focus on social reform and disaster relief operations. He has also been interested in supporting education and children's well-being through his humanitarian efforts.

One such example is his assistance for the "Children's Health Fund," a charity giving medical care to disadvantaged children. Cruise's engagement has brought attention and resources to the cause, indicating his determination to make a good influence beyond the silver screen.

In conclusion, Tom Cruise's personal life has been a tapestry of relationships, struggles, and obligations. His marriages and high-profile romances give an insight into the difficulty of juggling celebrity and intimacy. The delicate balance between his public image and his private world reveals the complex aspect of his existence. Moreover, his humanitarian initiatives indicate his dedication to utilizing his power for real change in the world.

CHAPTER 5

STUNTS AND ACTIONS

The Evolution of Tom Cruise

Tom Cruise's road to becoming the archetypal action star is a tale of change and determination. While his early career saw him flourish in a range of roles, he determined to push his limitations which pushed him toward being identified with heart-pounding action.

Cruise's first noteworthy moves into the action genre were seen in the 1986 picture "Top Gun." As Lieutenant Pete "Maverick" Mitchell, he went to the skies in adrenaline-pumping dogfights, displaying his desire to immerse himself in hard physical tasks. This significant job signaled the beginning of a trajectory that would reshape his career.

However, it was with the "Mission: Impossible" series that Cruise secured his image as a bona fide action star. The franchise's popularity hinges in great part on his devotion to doing his stunts. Cruise's devotion to authenticity is obvious in each movie, as he jumps buildings, dangles from helicopters, and engages in high-speed chases. This approach not only enhances the stakes of the movie but also displays his desire to give fans an unsurpassed watching experience.

Cruise's progress as an action star isn't only about doing stunts; it's about stretching emotional limits too. In "Collateral," he evolved into a vicious hitman, displaying his flexibility by portraying a complicated character within the framework of an action thriller. This holistic approach underlines his intention to keep audiences interested intellectually and emotionally, even in the middle of heart-racing action.

As Cruise continues to mature in the action genre, his drive for authenticity and inventiveness remains steadfast. His willingness to put himself in the thick of danger for cinematic reality has not only upped the standard for action films but also established his position in Hollywood history. The development of Tom Cruise, the action star, is an unending tale of ambition, reinvention, and a brave pursuit of the remarkable.

From Mission Impossible to Top Gun

Tom Cruise's oeuvre offers a plethora of jaw-dropping stunt scenes that have become unforgettable moments in cinematic history. From "Mission: Impossible" to "Top Gun," his determination to complete these stunning feats personally has set him apart as a brave and remarkable performer.

In the "Mission: Impossible" series, Cruise has repeatedly pushed the frontier of what's possible in action filmmaking. One notable moment from "Mission: Impossible – Ghost Protocol" depicts Cruise hanging to the outside of the Burj Khalifa, the world's tallest structure. This vertigo-inducing sequence demonstrates his passion for reality and his determination to tackle danger head-on. Similarly, in "Mission: Impossible – Fallout," the halo leap scene, executed over 100 times for the right picture, illustrates his rigorous attention to detail and his drive to create unprecedented visual spectacles.

"Top Gun," the picture that confirmed Cruise's star status, also featured outstanding stunt sequences. The high-octane aerial action scenes were produced with a combination of realistic effects and cutting-edge technology. Cruise's willingness to endure hard training to effectively represent a fighter pilot turned into a visceral watching experience that reflected the ferocity of aerial battle.

Cruise's devotion to these spectacular stunt scenes goes beyond the screen; it's a tribute to his appreciation for the profession and his desire to bring true excitement to his audience. These sequences are more than simply action; they're a reflection of his devotion to pushing the boundaries of cinema and generating moments that reverberate long after the credits roll.

The Physical Demands of Stunt Work

Tom Cruise's image as a daring action star isn't only the consequence of on-screen magic; it's the conclusion of his persistent dedication to pushing his physical and mental limitations in search of authenticity. Behind the scenes, the grueling world of stunt work becomes a monument to his commitment.

Cruise's propensity to complete his stunts is not without its hurdles. For instance, the "Mission: Impossible" series needs hard training and demanding physical fitness.

Whether it's studying difficult choreography for combat scenes or mastering new talents like high-speed motorbike riding, Cruise's tenacity comes through. He has been known to commit months to perfecting abilities that sometimes take years to perfect.

The toll of such physical exertion is visible in his injuries. During the filming of "Mission: Impossible – Fallout," Cruise injured his ankle while attempting a rooftop leap. Despite the setback, he returned to complete the scene after healing, a tribute to his perseverance and devotion to retaining the quality of his performances.

Cruise's devotion to pushing limits also extends to his partnership with stunt teams. He works together with experts that share his enthusiasm for authenticity and creativity.

Their partnership has resulted in innovative moments that redefine what's possible in action movies.

Ultimately, the physical rigors of stunt work in Tom Cruise's films transcend the silver screen. They show his unrelenting devotion to narrative, his quest for quality, and his determination to tackle obstacles head-on. Cruise's capacity to push himself beyond limitations is a reflection of his indomitable spirit and his devotion to creating entertainment that resonates emotionally with people.

CHAPTER 6

SCIENTOLOGY AND BELIEFS

Scientology's Influence on Tom Cruise's Career Choices

Tom Cruise's association with Scientology has been a persistent force affecting his job decisions and personal values. The Church of Scientology, founded by L. Ron Hubbard, advocates spiritual enlightenment and self-improvement via a series of practices and teachings. Cruise's introduction to Scientology in the early 1990s represented a turning point in his life since it brought about a fundamental transformation in his outlook.

Scientology's emphasis on human progress and potential connected strongly with

Cruise's ambitious character. He grew increasingly active in the Church's operations and even thanked Scientology for his success. The Church's doctrines inspire self-confidence and goal-setting, attributes that coincide with Cruise's passion for his trade.

As his engagement with Scientology developed, Cruise's work choices began to mirror his newfound convictions. He took on roles that repeated themes of personal development, perseverance, and questioning society's standards. These assignments often paralleled the ideas of Scientology, increasing his dedication to the church and allowing him to explore its themes via his profession.

Public Perception and Handling Controversies

Tom Cruise's affiliation with Scientology produced both adoration and scandal. His passionate public affirmations of Scientology techniques and his promotion of its advantages led to a diversity of attitudes. While many appreciated his fervor for his convictions, others voiced concerns about his influence and the procedures of the Church.

Controversies developed when Cruise stated opinions that were unusual or in conflict with prevailing attitudes. His passionate advocacy of Scientology's ideals during media interviews frequently led to public disagreements and heated arguments. These scandals periodically overshadowed his film releases and created problems for his public image.

Cruise's attitude to tackling these situations was one of conviction. He remained consistent in his ideas, frequently opting to face disagreements head-on rather than sidestepping them. His desire to participate in open dialogues revealed his dedication to his religion and helped him to bridge the gap between his personal life and his public image.

The Intersection of Faith and Fame

The junction of Tom Cruise's faith and stardom is a dynamic interaction that has shaped his public character. His reputation as a Hollywood icon heightened the emphasis on his participation in Scientology. This focus came both criticism and intrigue, as fans and detractors attempted to understand how his beliefs informed his decisions. Cruise's ability to blend his popularity with his faith has been a tribute to his unshakable dedication. He managed the difficulty of integrating his famous profile with the private character of his views. His attempts to preserve sincerity and participate in meaningful dialogues about his beliefs revealed his passion for spreading understanding and tolerance.

The combination of faith and stardom, unique to Tom Cruise, became a part of his legacy. His path served as a case study of how a public personality may incorporate their convictions into their public image while preserving a sense of integrity. The continual investigation of this delicate balance continues to impact the perspective of both Tom Cruise the actor and Tom Cruise the Scientologist.

CHAPTER 7

EVOLUTION OF STYLE

Tom Cruise as a Fashion Icon

Tom Cruise's path from his breakout performance in "Risky Business" to gracing the red carpets of premieres and award presentations has been distinguished by his growing sense of style. With a good eye for fashion, he turned his image from a youthful, fresh-faced actor to a global fashion hero.

In "Risky Business," Tom's character Joel Goodson's laid-back yet effortlessly sophisticated manner connected with moviegoers. The now-iconic scene of him dancing in a dress shirt and underpants exhibited a feeling of young disobedience that would become synonymous with his early character. This brave gesture not only established his persona but also created the groundwork for his stylistic trajectory.

As Tom's career climbed, his dress choices altered. He easily shifted from casual and comfortable clothes to finely fitted suits and tuxedos. His participation in films like "Top Gun" and "Rain Man" highlighted his ability to command attention on-screen not just with his acting abilities, but also with his sartorial choices. The aviator sunglasses in "Top Gun" were an enduring icon of his Maverick persona, while his classic outfits in "Rain Man" displayed his ability to exude refinement.

The Impact of His Iconic Looks on Pop Culture

Tom Cruise's wardrobe choices transcended the silver screen, making an enduring effect on pop culture. From the advent of the "Top Gun" bomber jacket fashion to the return of the aviator sunglasses, his effect rippled beyond the bounds of movie theaters. His distinctive smile, along with carefully picked clothing, established a pattern for how performers might wield their style as an instrument of persuasion.

The 80s and 90s saw an invasion of Cruise-inspired fashion trends, with individuals throughout the world embracing his leather jackets, white shirts, and wayfarer eyewear. His blend of casual and upmarket components disrupted established fashion rules, motivating a generation to experiment with their outfits.

The Tom Cruise Effect

Often referred to as the "Tom Cruise effect," his stylistic choices have continuously created trends and altered the fashion world. His ability to smoothly transition from action hero to stylish leading man has proven him a source of inspiration for designers, stylists, and fashion fans alike.

From his sleek outfits in the "Mission: Impossible" trilogy to his beautiful red carpet appearances, Cruise's wardrobe path exhibits versatility and adaptability. Designers often aim to emulate his feeling of timelessness by adding aspects from his classic designs into their collections. The Cruise effect isn't just about duplicating his attire; it's about capturing his confidence and charm, infusing items with a hint of that Cruise-like attraction.

In conclusion, Tom Cruise's rise as a fashion icon is a tribute to his ability to use clothes as a way of self-expression. From his early rebellious days to his polished red carpet-moments, he has reinvented what it means to be a Hollywood star with a style that resonates well beyond the big screen. His impact on fashion continues to inspire individuals to defy boundaries and embrace their distinct sense of style.

CHAPTER 8

FILMOGRAPHY ANALYSIS

Character Transformations

Tom Cruise's career displays his outstanding skill for taking on varied roles and enduring substantial character shifts. Let's look at the intricacies of how he has expertly navigated through numerous individuals, each distinct in their personality, goals, and challenges:

1. Vincent in "Collateral" (2004)

In "Collateral," Cruise portrays Vincent, a contract murderer. This shift from his normal heroic roles allowed Cruise to exhibit his flexibility. Vincent's cold and calculating personality contrasts strikingly with Cruise's gregarious presence. Through subtle facial expressions and body language, Cruise evolves into a frightening adversary, exploring the nuances of a morally ambiguous figure.

2. Lestat in "Interview with the Vampire" (1994)

Playing Lestat, a centuries-old vampire, Cruise produced a captivating yet frightening performance. He embraced the character's dark appeal and emotional problems, depicting both the draw of immortality and the weight of endless loneliness. Cruise's transition into Lestat highlighted his ability to depict complicated, otherworldly creatures while yet preserving a feeling of humanity inside the part.

3. Charlie Babbitt in "Rain Man" (1988)

In "Rain Man," Cruise played Charlie Babbitt, a self-centered person who finds that his estranged brother is an autistic savant. Cruise's depiction highlights his progress as an actor, as he transforms from a self-absorbed hustler to a sympathetic brother. His character evolution represents the journey of knowledge and empathy, allowing Cruise to explore the emotional depth of Charlie's internal transformations.

4. Jerry Maguire in "Jerry Maguire" (1996)

As Jerry Maguire, a sports agent who suffers a crisis of conscience and sets out to build a new sort of agency, Cruise offers a multi-layered performance. He evolves from a loud, success-driven agent to a guy seeking sincerity and meaningful connections. Cruise's portrayal depicts the maturation of

Jerry's ideals and objectives, displaying his ability to represent individuals enduring tremendous inner change.

5. Ethan Hunt in the "Mission: Impossible" Series (1996 - Present)

Tom Cruise's portrayal of Ethan Hunt throughout numerous films is a masterpiece in continuous character progression. From the first film to the newest movie, Cruise turns Hunt from a capable though sometimes impetuous agent to a seasoned commander who mixes action with strategic thinking. Cruise's devotion to completing his own stunts lends a depth of reality to the character's physical metamorphosis, showcasing Hunt's toughness and flexibility.

Tom Cruise's exceptional ability to immerse himself in a broad range of personalities proves his devotion to his art. With each part, he not only demonstrates his acting talent but also explores the complex nuances of human nature, delivering performances that touch emotionally with viewers and solidifying his position as one of Hollywood's most versatile performers.

Analyzing Top Gun and its Legacy

In the domain of cinematic history, there exists a unique breed of film that not only creates a genre but also etches its protagonist into the public mind. "Top Gun," published in 1986, serves as a highlight in the career of Tom Cruise, placing him into a position that would mold his image as the personification of the maverick persona.

The film's plot centers around Pete "Maverick" Mitchell, a daring and highly competent fighter pilot who feeds on danger and possesses an unshakable dedication to his trade. The character's rebellious attitude, unrelenting resolve, and fearsome aptitude epitomize the attributes that would eventually become synonymous with Cruise's movie presence.

"Maverick" Mitchell's path is one of self-discovery as much as it is about aerial talent. His tenacious pursuit of brilliance in the face of difficult odds symbolizes the determination that Cruise would bring to his following roles. Maverick's conflicts with authority, his affinity with fellow pilots, and his nuanced dance with danger all add to the multiple layers that distinguish Cruise's depiction.

What sets "Top Gun" aside from being a mere action film is its superb combination of exciting airborne scenes and deep character development. The romantic subplot between Maverick and his instructor, Charlie, displays fragility underneath the façade of invincibility, further cementing Maverick as a complex figure.

The film's influence is not restricted to its initial effect; rather, it spreads across the fabric of popular culture. The term "maverick" itself has developed to include persons who enjoy nonconformity and bravery. The aircraft scenes, expertly coordinated and superbly photographed, set a benchmark that echoes in current action filmmaking.

Furthermore, the Maverick identity kindled by Cruise's performance has woven its way into his future parts. Whether it's Ethan Hunt in the "Mission: Impossible" series or the flamboyant sports agent Jerry Maguire, vestiges of Maverick's dauntless energy are unmistakable, acting as the center of Cruise's on-screen charm.

In essence, "Top Gun" solidified Tom Cruise's professional trajectory, carving the Maverick identity into the tapestry of film history. The film's unashamed daring, its celebration of friendship and uniqueness, and its representation of the exhilaration and risks of pushing limits have established its place as a timeless masterpiece. As viewers continue to be enthralled by Maverick's daring flying maneuvers and emotional turmoil, the film's legacy drives onward, a monument to the lasting power of a distinct cinematic representation.

Tom Cruise in Drama and Sci-Fi

Tom Cruise's voyage across the realms of drama and science fiction on the silver screen has been nothing short of enthralling. From his earliest performances to his current ventures, Cruise's ability to immerse himself in complicated characters and traverse difficult narratives has displayed his flexibility as an actor.

Diving into Dramatic Complexity

In the domain of drama, Tom Cruise has continually established himself as an actor capable of digging into the depths of human emotion. His portrayal of emotionally charged characters has shown his variety and devotion to the narrative. Consider his performance in "Rain Man," when he starred opposite Dustin Hoffman. Cruise's performance as Charlie Babbitt, a self-absorbed guy who learns compassion from his autistic brother, demonstrated a degree of vulnerability and realism that made an unforgettable imprint.

Another example comes in "A Few Good Men," when Cruise steps into the shoes of Lieutenant Daniel Kaffee, a defense attorney uncovering a convoluted military plot. The film's tough courtroom sequences allowed Cruise to exhibit his expertise in mixing appeal with the solemnity necessary to address ethical concerns.

Venturing into the Unknown: Cruise in Sci-Fi

When it comes to science fiction, Cruise's passion for his art is equally clear. He courageously explores unexplored territory, embracing the speculative and the futuristic with unyielding determination. "Minority Report" remains a testament to his ability to mix action with mental depth. In the guise of Chief John Anderton, Cruise navigates a futuristic world where precrime is utilized to prevent murders. His complex presentation dives into questions like free choice and the ethical consequences of technology.

Furthermore, "Edge of Tomorrow" places Cruise in a time-loop scenario, representing Major William Cage. The film's sophisticated narrative and character development needed Cruise to depict a character shifting from hesitancy to heroism. His path inside the movie matches his real-life devotion to breaking boundaries and exploring unexplored ground in his acting profession.

A Confluence of Drama and Sci-Fi

What sets Cruise apart is his ability to fluidly segue between drama and science fiction, emphasizing the interconnectivity of human emotion and theoretical notions. His performances are a testimony to the concept that rich characters and sophisticated storytelling need not be bound to one genre.

In exploring Cruise's parts in drama and science fiction, we unearth a tapestry of performances that reflect his devotion to his craft, his desire to push himself, and his profound knowledge of the human experience.

CHAPTER 9

FAN CULTURE

How Tom Cruise's Fans Have Evolved

Over the decades, Tom Cruise's followers have experienced a remarkable development, matching the shifts in media consumption, technology, and societal dynamics. From his early days as a budding star to his standing as a Hollywood legend, Cruise's fan base has shifted in parallel with his professional trajectory. In the 1980s, fans mostly depended on periodicals, television appearances, and movie screenings to connect with their idol. The fan culture was more localized, with fan clubs and mailing lists functioning as the major centers for communication.

As the digital era emerged in the 1990s and 2000s, the relationship between Cruise and his followers began to shift radically. Internet forums and early social media platforms allowed followers to interact internationally, surpassing geographical barriers. This era witnessed the growth of fan websites dedicated to examining his work, analyzing his performances, and digging into his personal life. The fans were becoming more active players, creating information and giving insights that would affect the way Cruise's career was regarded.

Fan Theories and Fan-Made Content

The rise of fan theories and fan-made content represented a crucial turning point in how Tom Cruise's followers connected with his work. As his filmography increased, viewers started to scrutinize the subtleties of his characters and themes, often diving further into the tales than even the filmmakers themselves. Mission Impossible, with its complicated storylines and turns, provided a fertile field for fan conjecture.

Alongside hypotheses, fan-made content gained momentum. From imaginative reinterpretations of events to wholly new narratives, fans exhibited their love through fan literature, artwork, and even fan-edited movies. These emotions not only represented the fans' enthusiasm but also indicated their emotional commitment to Cruise's movie universe. The rising accessibility of digital resources makes it feasible for fans to harness their creativity and share their contributions on online platforms, building a feeling of community.

The Global Reach of Tom Cruise Fandom

In recent years, the global spread of Tom Cruise fandom has been illustrated by the expansion of events and online groups. From San Diego Comic-Con to specific gatherings like "CruiseCon," fans from over the world flock to honor his achievements. These meetings allow fans the opportunity to meet like-minded folks, engage with special material, and occasionally even interact with the man himself.

Online communities have become crucial to the fan experience, connecting fans across countries quickly. Social media sites, notably Twitter and Instagram, have become virtual fan centers where followers share news, review films, and celebrate Cruise's triumphs.

Facebook groups and Reddit communities provide areas for in-depth conversations and collaborative initiatives.

In conclusion, Tom Cruise's fanbase has gone from magazine cutouts and local fan groups to a global network of networked devotees. It has developed from passive adoration to active involvement, encouraging a culture of innovation and cooperation. Cruise's ability to adapt to changing circumstances, along with the loyalty of his followers, has established his position not just in the history of cinema but also in the annals of fan culture progression.

CHAPTER 10

CONTROVERSIES AND COMEBACKS

Tom Cruise's Public Interviews and Image Challenges

Tom Cruise's path through the media environment has been both enthralling and difficult. His contacts with the media have often been examined, with incidents that vary from adorable to problematic. One of the most notorious incidents was the infamous 2005 interview with Oprah Winfrey, where he boldly confessed his love for Katie Holmes by leaping on her couch. This impulsive outburst, however sincere, prompted extensive suspicion about his behavior and personal life. The event underlined how even the most seemingly benign gestures by celebrities can be amplified and sensationalized in the media.

Cruise's approach to resolving media difficulties demonstrates his drive to control his story. In reaction to criticism and conjecture, he has adopted techniques such as carefully managed public appearances, strategic interviews, and social media involvement. These initiatives have tried to restore control of his public image and shift the debate toward his professional successes and charity pursuits.

Career Resilience

Tom Cruise's career has been a rollercoaster journey, defined by both amazing achievements and surprising downturns. Despite being one of the greatest performers in Hollywood, he has endured moments where his popularity dropped owing to a mix of causes, including box office failures and scandals. One of the most prominent career drops came during the mid-2000s when a succession of lackluster films and controversial public episodes prompted some to question his star power.

What sets Cruise different is his amazing ability to come back and reshape his career. He continuously exhibits perseverance by adopting varied parts that test him as an actor. For instance, his depiction as Les Grossman in "Tropic Thunder" was a break from his customary leading man demeanor, displaying his willingness to take chances and embrace self-parody.

Cruise's victorious comeback may be due to his devotion to developing his craft and cooperating with imaginative filmmakers who understand his potential. His work with Christopher McQuarrie in the "Mission: Impossible" franchise epitomizes this dynamic. Through great attention to his physical preparation and a willingness to engage in hazardous stunts, Cruise rejuvenated his career by remaking himself as an action hero with unrivaled commitment.

In conclusion, Tom Cruise's path through scandals and career swings illustrates his capacity to adapt, alter, and remain relevant in a dynamic profession. His smart media navigation and persistent devotion to his craft have secured his place as an enduring Hollywood legend.

How Controversies Shape the Tom Cruise Narrative

Tom Cruise's career has been distinguished by a succession of incidents, each playing a significant part in molding the narrative around his public image and professional trajectory. These disputes are more than simply bumps on the road; they have added to the richness of his image and the public's view of him.

1. Couch-Jumping event (2005): The infamous couch-jumping event on "The Oprah Winfrey Show" became a defining moment. Cruise's passionate expression of adoration for then-girlfriend Katie Holmes was viewed with both laughter and anxiety. This issue converted Cruise from an attractive actor into a topic of derision, ruining his image as a

composed superstar. It represented a change in public image and prompted issues about the authenticity of his feelings.

2. Scientology and Public Words: Cruise's involvement with Scientology and his public words advocating for the controversial religion have ignited controversy. His ardent support of Scientology's tactics has led to both praise and mistrust. This debate has weaved itself into his story, making talks about his beliefs a vital component of any conversation about his life and work.

3. Relationships and Marriages: Cruise's high-profile marriages, particularly with Nicole Kidman and Katie Holmes, have given fodder for tabloids and gossip columns. The supposition around these relationships has become inseparable from his story, adding a

dimension of interest and curiosity to his personal life. These issues have underlined the difficulty of keeping a private life in the public glare.

4. Public Image and Professionalism: Several instances of unpredictable conduct and difficult confrontations with the media have contributed to an image of Cruise as a volatile personality. His impassioned defense of his principles and aggressive personality have both drawn love and condemnation. These disputes have contributed complexity to his public image, depicting him as a multi-dimensional character with strong convictions.

5. Mission: Impossible Franchise and Stunt Work: Cruise's devotion to completing his own stunts, although lauded, has also been

regarded with worry for his safety. The debates around the risks he takes and the possible impact on his health have given a dimension of suspense to his action-packed parts. This tale demonstrates his unrelenting devotion to his work and the extent he takes to provide authenticity to his audience.

In each of these cases, the issues have played a significant part in molding the narrative of Tom Cruise's life and career. They have proved his capacity to withstand storms, adjust to shifting views, and emerge stronger than before. Rather than hindrances, these conflicts have become important pieces in the fabric of his legacy, giving richness and authenticity to the tale of an actor who continues to enchant audiences worldwide.

CONCLUSION

Tom Cruise stands as a luminary who has not only survived the ever-shifting waves of fame but has also irrevocably engraved his name into the annals of cinematic brilliance. His path from a young aspirant to a famous figure has been nothing short of a symphony, crafted with effort, brilliance, and unwavering desire.

As we explore the pages of this book, we've exposed the many layers that compose the essence of Tom Cruise. From his early attempts into the domain of acting to his spectacular climb to prominence, Cruise's history reveals a persistence that has catapulted him above the ordinary. Each job he has played, and each character he has represented, has added to an ever-evolving mosaic that characterizes his legacy.

His significance surpasses ordinary entertainment, as he has left an enduring mark on popular culture and cultural conventions. The charming aura he emanates isn't only a façade but an expression of an artist's passion for his work. Cruise's impact has extended across continents, affecting the lives of countless followers who have drawn inspiration from his path of self-discovery, reinvention, and unrelenting pursuit of perfection.

Yet, in our research, we have also negotiated the labyrinthine disputes that have interrupted his career. A life lived under the constant glare of the limelight attracts scrutiny, and Cruise's ability to manage these stormy seas has demonstrated a tenacity that parallels his characters' unflinching drive. Through trials, he has risen not as an ordinary survivor but as a phoenix, flying to even higher heights.

In this climax, we are reminded that Tom Cruise's journey is not a finite tale but a continuous narrative that continues to expand with every new endeavor, every honor gained, and every threshold he dares to break. The last curtain call of this novel is not a closing act but a painful pause, allowing readers to watch the chapters still to be written.

The Power of Persistence

In Tom Cruise's journey, we learn that patience is the cornerstone of success. He experienced early rejections and failures but refused to give up on his aspirations. Each rejection just spurred his drive to prove himself. This reminds us that in our own lives, tenacity in the face of adversity may take us to our desired goals. When we confront hurdles, we may draw inspiration from Cruise's narrative and keep pushing forward, knowing that tenacity can convert aspirations into reality.

Embracing Fear as Fuel

Tom Cruise's daring acts remind us that fear can be a tremendous source of drive. Rather than shying away from fear, he embraced it as a driving force to climb new heights. This method pushes us to accept our worries and convert them into catalysts for progress. Just as Cruise courageously takes on challenging maneuvers, we may attack our obstacles with renewed boldness, realizing that venturing out of our comfort zones can lead to extraordinary successes.

Balance Amidst Stardom

Cruise's ability to retain equilibrium among the flash and glamour of Hollywood emphasizes the necessity of grounding oneself in the middle of success. His devotion to family and personal beliefs indicates that despite celebrity, being true to one's convictions and loved ones is crucial. This lesson teaches us to develop a firm foundation of integrity and humility even when faced with accolades. By valuing what genuinely matters, we may negotiate the pull of prosperity without compromising our identity.

The Art of Reinvention

Throughout his career, Tom Cruise has proved the power of reinvention. From serious performances to action-packed blockbusters, he's demonstrated his flexibility over and again. This reminds us that accepting change and adjusting to new difficulties is crucial for personal progress. Just as Cruise accepted numerous jobs, we should be open to acquiring new talents, exploring new pathways, and expanding ourselves. The skill of reinvention helps us to continually broaden our horizons and stay relevant in a changing environment.

Resilience in Adversity

Tom Cruise's ability to bounce back from scandals and losses illustrates the strength of perseverance. Rather than letting setbacks define him, he used them as stepping stones toward future accomplishments. This lesson reminds us that setbacks are part of any journey, and our attitude to them defines our destiny. By adopting Cruise's resilience, we may weather storms, learn from setbacks, and emerge stronger, recognizing that adversity can be a platform for development and eventual success.

Inspiring Through Action

Cruise's willingness to execute his stunts shows leadership by example. He inspires by his deeds, proving that devotion and hard effort are the pillars of influence. This lesson inspires us to be leaders in our own lives by exhibiting our devotion to our goals. By putting in the effort and leading with action, we may influence others to follow suit and have a good impact on the world around us.

The Rewards of Risk-Taking

Tom Cruise's willingness to take calculated chances in his profession and stunts reminds us that measured risks can lead to remarkable achievements. While not every risk assures success, a well-calculated bet might bring unexpected benefits. Cruise's narrative challenges us to analyze risks, venture outside our comfort zones, and seek undertakings that can uplift us. Through careful risk-taking, we may find hidden skills, establish new routes, and gain the advantages of stepping beyond the conventional.

Authenticity Amidst Expectations

Cruise's ability to maintain authenticity despite society's standards shows us the virtue of keeping true to ourselves. In a profession generally distinguished by uniformity, he's constantly selected positions that resonate with him, keeping genuine to his convictions. This lesson inspires us to resist the impulse to conform and instead embrace our originality. By being loyal to our ideas, interests, and unique viewpoints, we may construct a meaningful path that corresponds with our actual selves.

A Journey of Continuous Learning

From drama to action, Tom Cruise's devotion to studying and mastering varied roles illustrates the significance of lifelong learning. His commitment to consistently developing and polishing his skill serves as a reminder that progress is a lifetime endeavor. This lesson urges us to approach life with an attitude of continual learning. By searching out new knowledge, skills, and experiences, we may improve our lives and preserve a feeling of wonder and curiosity that pulls us forward.

Impact Through Positive Influence

Through his films and activities, Tom Cruise has made a lasting impression on audiences throughout the world. His narrative shows us that our acts, no matter how tiny, can impact and inspire others. Just like Cruise's devotion to his trade has left a mark, we may create a good effect with our hobbies, activities, and relationships. By recognizing our ability to uplift people around us, we may contribute to a more caring and inspired world.

Acknowledgments

Behind every masterpiece, numerous hands contribute to its production. The tapestry of this book has been created with threads of inspiration, advice, and cooperation, each strand contributing to its richness and depth.

I send my deepest thanks to all whose thoughts and wisdom have brightened this path. To the individuals who have graciously shared their tales, providing light on the riddle of Tom Cruise, I am sincerely obliged. Your willingness to give your thoughts has brought levels of authenticity to our venture.

My admiration also goes to the unsung heroes—the researchers, editors, and advisors—who have assiduously worked to assure the authenticity and resonance of this tale. Your devotion has been the basis upon which this exploration stands.

Lastly, to the readers that go on this expedition, thank you for embarking on this trip of discovery. May the pages you flip show not simply the biography of an actor but the universal narrative of a human being navigating the kaleidoscope of fame, ambition, and the constant pursuit of passion.

In the combination of conclusion and recognition, we discover not an end but a continuation—an emotion that parallels the continuous journey of the man who has been at the core of this tale.

Printed in Great Britain
by Amazon

First published in 2006 by
Carlton Books Limited
20 Mortimer Street
London W1T 3JW

Copyright ©2006 Carlton Books Limited

Arsenal.com

A CIP catalogue record for this book is available
from the British Library.

ISBN-10: 1-84442-256-9
ISBN-13: 978-1-84442-256-2

Editorial Manager: Roland Hall
Project Art Director: Darren Jordan
Design: Ben Ruocco
Picture Research: Tom Wright/Paul Langan
Gunnersaurus illustration (pp 52–53): Des Taylor
Production: Lisa French

Printed in Italy

The Publishers would like to thank the following sources for their kind
permission to reproduce the pictures in this book: Empics: /Jon Buckle: 19
(col. 2 pic. 5); /David Davies/PA: 19 (col. 1 pic. 3), 19 (col. 2 pic. 2), 19 (col.
1 pic. 4); /Sean Dempsey/PA: 19 (col. 2 pic. 3); /Matt Dunham/AP: 19 (col. 1
pic. 2); /David Jones/PA: 37t; /PA: 48t

All other images kindly supplied by Arsenal Football Club: Photographers
Stuart MacFarlane and David Price

The Official
Arsenal
Annual 2007

Chas Newkey-Burden

CARLTON BOOKS

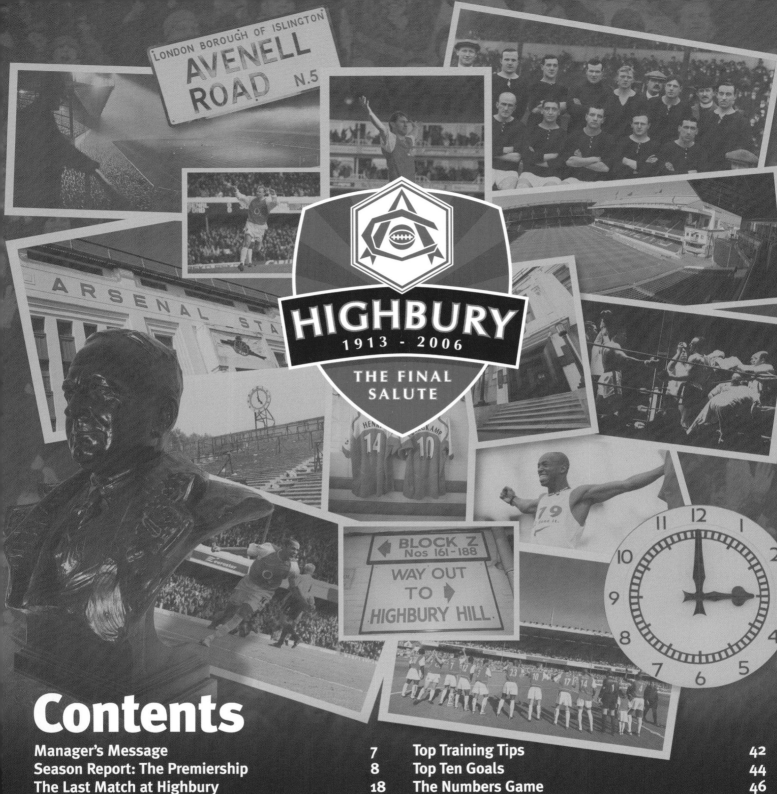

Contents

Dear Supporters,

Welcome to the Official Arsenal Annual 2007.

The season just passed has been extremely eventful, culminating in the Champions League Final in Paris, which was a night of disappointment but also of pride for everyone associated with Arsenal Football Club. I have no doubt that we can go one better in the forthcoming season and lift the trophy.

The trail to Paris was one of the most impressive and enjoyable footballing campaigns I have ever been part of. I feel we grew throughout the competition, but the victory away to Real Madrid was the turning point. From that game onwards, I really believed we could go all the way and reach the Final.

Although we were disappointed to finish only fourth in the Premiership, we are delighted to have secured Champions League football for next season, and the way we secured it on the final day of the season was very dramatic. What a fitting way to sign off from Highbury!

I feel we are at the beginning of a new era for the Club. We have our new home at the Emirates Stadium and an exceptional team with a number of enormously talented young players in its ranks. The future seems very bright for the Club.

I would like to thank the Arsenal supporters for their incredible support throughout the 2005/2006 season. Even during some testing times, you stuck by us and your backing was, of course, instrumental in our successes during the campaign. I hope you will enjoy the Official Arsenal Annual 2007. It is a fantastic document of some very exciting times at a very special football club.

Thanks again for your support,

Arsène Wenger

Arsenal kicked off their Premiership campaign with a new captain, a new coloured kit and three points from their opening fixture.

AUGUST 2005

The 2–0 victory over Newcastle United did not come easily – both goals were in the final nine minutes – but it was thoroughly deserved. The first goal of the campaign came from the new captain, Thierry Henry. Freddie Ljungberg was fouled in the area and Henry side-footed the resulting penalty past Shay Given. Substitute Robin Van Persie tied things up six minutes later when he scored from the near post after fine work from Ljungberg.

This was followed by a trip to Stamford Bridge where, but for a bizarre goal from Didier Drogba, Arsenal would have come away with at least a point after a close game. Alexander Hleb made his Premiership debut in Arsène Wenger's 500th game as Arsenal manager and, along with his team-mates, put on an impressive display. However, in the 73rd minute Drogba tried to control a pass from Frank Lampard and inadvertently scored after the ball bounced off his knee.

> ❝IT FEELS GREAT BECAUSE IF THE SUPPORTERS ARE SINGING YOUR NAME IT MEANS YOU HAVE DONE YOUR JOB.❞
>
> **PASCAL CYGAN**

Not many Arsenal matches end with two players chasing a hat-trick and fewer still end with Pascal Cygan being one of those players. But the 4–1 victory over Fulham was not 'many matches'. The game started badly when Lauren missed a penalty and then Claus Jensen put the visitors ahead with a fine chip. But two goals from Cygan and two from Henry gave the Gunners all three points.

AUGUST 14, 2005 ARSENAL 2–0 NEWCASTLE UNITED
(HENRY 81, VAN PERSIE 87)
AUGUST 21, 2005 CHELSEA 1–0 ARSENAL
AUGUST 24, 2005 ARSENAL 4–1 FULHAM
(CYGAN 32, 90, HENRY 53, 82)

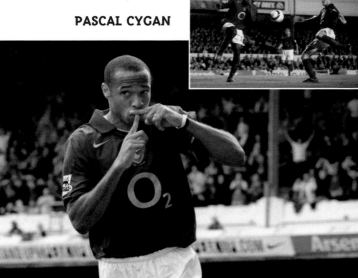

SEPTEMBER 2005

A mixed month for Arsenal began at the Riverside Stadium, often a happy hunting ground for the Gunners – but not on this occasion.

The visitors created a lot of chances but failed to capitalise on them. Jose Antonio Reyes hit a post early on and Arsenal had a strong shout for a penalty. However, Arsène Wenger's men only emerged with a late consolation goal from Reyes after Middlesbrough had scored twice either side of the break.

With two defeats already to their name, Arsenal took to the field against Everton in determined mood. In the previous home match Cygan had scored twice, and his central defensive partner Sol Campbell repeated that feat against the Toffees. Both goals were headers from Jose Antonio Reyes free-kicks and sealed a satisfying victory for the home fans.

The Everton victory put Arsenal one place below West Ham United in the table but the Gunners were unable to capitalise on this when they visited Upton Park. With Thierry Henry injured, Reyes led the attack and came close on a number of occasions. Arsenal – and, most notably, Cesc Fabregas – performed well, but were not able to grab a winner so had to share the points with the Hammers.

SEPTEMBER 10, 2005 MIDDLESBROUGH 2–1 ARSENAL
(REYES 90)
SEPTEMBER 19, 2005 ARSENAL 2–0 EVERTON
(CAMPBELL 11, 30)
SEPTEMBER 24, 2005 WEST HAM UNITED 0–0 ARSENAL

> ❝AS DENNIS BERGKAMP SAID, 'WE NEED TO PLAY LIKE A TEAM'. YOU WIN AS A TEAM AND YOU LOSE AS AN INDIVIDUAL. ❞
>
> **THIERRY HENRY**

> ❝IT WAS IMPORTANT TO WIN AGAINST EVERTON AND I FEEL WE DID IT WELL AND IN A CONTROLLED WAY. WE SCORED TWO UNUSUAL GOALS FROM SET PIECES. I FEEL THE TEAM IS BACK FOCUSED, WITH BELIEF, DISCIPLINE AND SHARPNESS. ❞
>
> **ARSENE WENGER**

OCTOBER 2005

An inconsistent month for Arsenal saw the team collect two wins, a draw and a loss, scoring once in each match.

The first victory came against Birmingham City, but the Gunners had to work really hard to collect all three points. Visiting goalkeeper Maik Taylor put in a vintage performance, blocking everything Arsenal threw at him – including a Robert Pires penalty. Then, in the 81st minute, substitute Robin Van Persie's speculative shot was deflected past him by Stephen Clemence.

> **" I FEEL POSITIVE BECAUSE WE CAME BACK AGAINST SPURS. IF THE GAME HAD GONE ON FOR FIVE OR TEN MINUTES MORE, THEN WE WOULD HAVE WON IT. "**
>
> **ARSENE WENGER**

An injury-hit Arsenal then travelled to The Hawthorns and went down to a shock 2–1 defeat. Philippe Senderos opened the scoring with his first goal for the Club, only for the home team to hit back with two strikes, including one by Arsenal old boy Nwankwo Kanu. This was Arsenal's third defeat of the season.

Better news emerged from the following Premiership game, at home to Manchester City. A Pires penalty in the 61st minute

sealed the points, but it was his second spot-kick which grabbed the headlines the following day. He tried to set up Thierry Henry from the spot but the venture went horribly wrong and led to a free-kick being awarded against the Gunners. However, when the full-time whistle blew, nobody could take Arsenal's win away from them.

And so to White Hart Lane where, thanks to Tottenham's improved form, this was one of the most hotly-anticipated North London derbies for years. When Ledley King gave the home side an early lead, Spurs fans scented victory. Pires came on as a half-time substitute and saved a point for Arsenal with a 77th-minute goal.

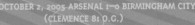

OCTOBER 2, 2005 ARSENAL 1–0 BIRMINGHAM CITY
(CLEMENCE 81 O.G.)
OCTOBER 15, 2005 WEST BROMWICH ALBION 2–1 ARSENAL
(SENDEROS 18)
OCTOBER 22, 2005 ARSENAL 1–0 MANCHESTER CITY
(PIRES 61 PEN)
OCTOBER 29, 2005 TOTTENHAM HOTSPUR 1–1 ARSENAL
(PIRES 77)

NOVEMBER 2005

November might have heralded the beginning of winter, but Arsenal fans were glowing throughout the month thanks to a 100 per cent record in the Premiership.

The first win came at home to Sunderland. A goal from Robin Van Persie and two from Thierry Henry sealed the team's eighth straight home victory of the season in all competitions. Alan Stubbs scored only the second goal the Gunners had conceded at Highbury in the Premiership this season.

Although Arsenal had suffered on their travels already this season, they came away from Wigan with all three points after a fantastic match at the JJB Stadium. Arsenal were ahead throughout the five-goal thriller but were

> **"THE WIGAN GAME WAS THE TYPE WHEN YOU SEE WHETHER YOU ARE A REAL PLAYER WHO IS READY TO PLAY IN THE ENGLISH LEAGUE."**
>
> **CESC FABREGAS**

made to work for their points. Again, the goals were shared between Van Persie and Henry as the Gunners won 3–2.

Thierry Henry scored his 100th league goal at Highbury during an entertaining win over Blackburn Rovers. Cesc Fabregas had opened the scoring in the fourth minute

NOVEMBER 5, 2005 ARSENAL 3–1 SUNDERLAND
(VAN PERSIE 12, HENRY 36, 82)
NOVEMBER 19, 2005 WIGAN ATHLETIC 2–3 ARSENAL
(VAN PERSIE 11, HENRY 21, 41)
NOVEMBER 26, 2005 ARSENAL 3–0 BLACKBURN ROVERS
(FABREGAS 4, HENRY 45, VAN PERSIE 90)

with a curled shot from 25 yards. Then, on the stroke of half-time, Henry ran onto a Pires pass and reached the landmark as he scored. The goal of the match – and perhaps the entire campaign – came in the final minute from Van Persie. The young Dutchman danced past two defenders and gloriously curled the ball home from a tight angle.

> **"WE HAVE TO STICK TO OUR USUAL GAME. WE WANT TO FOCUS ON OUR QUICK PASSING GAME AND GET THAT RIGHT. THAT'S THE PRIORITY."**
>
> **ARSENE WENGER**

> **"WE NEED TO HAVE A PHYSICAL SIDE TOO. WE HAVE TO LEARN THAT AND DEAL WITH IT."**
>
> **DENNIS BERGKAMP**

DECEMBER 3, 2005
BOLTON WANDERERS 2–0 ARSENAL
DECEMBER 10, 2005 NEWCASTLE UNITED 1–0 ARSENAL
DECEMBER 18, 2005 ARSENAL 0–2 CHELSEA
DECEMBER 26, 2005 CHARLTON ATHLETIC 0–1 ARSENAL
(REYES 58)
DECEMBER 28, 2005 ARSENAL 4–0 PORTSMOUTH
(BERGKAMP 7, REYES 13, HENRY 36, 42 PEN)
DECEMBER 31, 2005 ASTON VILLA 0–0 ARSENAL

DECEMBER 2005

A mixed month for Arsenal started with three defeats and no goals scored, but ended with two wins and a draw, with no goals conceded.

> **"IT IS A CONFIDENCE THING. I FEEL FOR A WHILE WE DID NOT KNOW, WE LOST A LITTLE BIT OF BELIEF THAT WE ARE THE BEST."**
>
> **ARSENE WENGER**

It began with a 2–0 defeat at Bolton, the Gunners' first defeat for ten games. Things could have been different were it not for second-half heroics from Bolton goalkeeper Jussi Jaaskelainen. Arsenal were unlucky to lose at St James' Park a week later. Once again they were thwarted by an in-form goalkeeper, this time Shay Given. And a trio of defeats was completed when defending champions Chelsea visited Highbury a week before Christmas and won 2–0.

The Gunners bounced back on Boxing Day. A fine performance at the Valley was capped by a goal by Jose Antonio Reyes to secure all three points against Charlton. Two days later, Portsmouth visited Highbury and were walloped 4–0 as the home team put on a hot performance on a cold winter night. Reyes scored again and was joined by Dennis Bergkamp and Thierry Henry (twice) on the scoresheet.

Although Arsenal's match at Villa Park ended 0–0, it was thoroughly entertaining. Mathieu Flamini, Freddie Ljungberg and Kolo Toure all went close, while Aston Villa also had some good chances. However, the last game in 2005 ended with Arsenal sharing the points.

JANUARY 2006

The new year began much as the old one ended, with inconsistent performances and a goalless draw.

First up was a visit from Manchester United. Highbury has witnessed some dramatic encounters between these two sides down the years, but the final clash between them at the stadium was a somewhat tame affair. Gilberto and Thierry Henry both came close and Cesc Fabregas had a good shout for a penalty turned down. The game ended all-square.

After going more than 180 minutes of Premiership football without scoring, the Arsenal floodgates opened against Middlesbrough. And then some. Henry scored his eighth Arsenal hat-trick and was joined on the crowded scoresheet by Philippe Senderos, Robert Pires, Gilberto and Alexander Hleb. A marvellous afternoon.

How Arsène Wenger must have wished he could transfer two of the goals from the Middlesbrough match to the clash at Goodison Park with Everton. The Gunners went 1-0 down to James Beattie's early strike and never recovered their composure enough to bounce back.

JANUARY 3, 2006 ARSENAL 0–0 MANCHESTER UNITED
JANUARY 7, 2006 ARSENAL 7–0 MIDDLESBROUGH
(HENRY 20, 30, 68, SENDEROS 22, PIRES 47,
GILBERTO 59, HLEB 84)
JANUARY 21, 2006 EVERTON 1–0 ARSENAL

❝WE COULD HAVE SCORED MORE AGAINST MIDDLESBROUGH. WE NOW HAVE TO TRANSFER THAT WEEK IN, WEEK OUT, AND BE CONSISTENT AGAIN. ❞

ARSENE WENGER

❝I THINK AS LONG AS THE TEAM DEFENDS WELL, WE MAKE IT EASIER FOR OURSELVES AND WE HAVE DONE THAT LATELY. ❞

LAUREN

FEBRUARY 2006

A win at Birmingham City was the highlight of a month which saw five points dropped at home and two defeats in the North-west.

The visit of West Ham United provided an evening of sheer drama at Highbury, but the home fans would have far preferred a dull match ending in a 1-0 victory. Midway through the first-half,

West Ham punished two defensive lapses to take a 2-0 lead. However, Henry's goal on the stroke of half-time offered hope. The game ended 3-2 after both sides scored once during the second-half.

At St Andrews, Arsenal won 2–0 against Birmingham City and both goals were significant in their different ways. Henry's was special as it marked his 200th strike for the Club. Emmanuel Adebayor, on the other hand, scored his first goal for the Gunners. The first of many it is to be hoped! This precious away win gave everyone at Highbury plenty to smile about.

Bolton Wanderers took the lead in the 12th minute at Highbury and looked set to hold onto their lead as Arsenal threw everything they had at them for the rest of the match. However, in injury time Fabregas crossed and his central midfield partner Gilberto smashed the ball home. A point saved. Arsenal emerged from their next two Premiership games without a point after Liverpool and Blackburn Rovers both beat them 1–0.

FEBRUARY 1, 2006
ARSENAL 2–3 WEST HAM UNITED
(HENRY 45, PIRES 89)
FEBRUARY 4, 2006 BIRMINGHAM CITY 0–2 ARSENAL
(ADEBAYOR 21, HENRY 63)
FEBRUARY 11, 2006 ARSENAL 1–1 BOLTON WANDERERS
(GILBERTO 90)
FEBRUARY 14, 2006 LIVERPOOL 1–0 ARSENAL
FEBRUARY 25, 2006
BLACKBURN ROVERS 1–0 ARSENAL

> **"DIABY WAS EXCELLENT AGAINST BIRMINGHAM CITY. HE IS STRONG, HE IS GOOD ON THE BALL, HE HAS A GREAT ENGINE FOR 90 MINUTES AND HE IS GOOD IN THE AIR AS WELL. IN EVERY GAME IT LOOKS LIKE HE IS GETTING STRONGER."**
>
> **ARSENE WENGER**

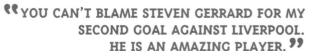
"YOU CAN'T BLAME STEVEN GERRARD FOR MY SECOND GOAL AGAINST LIVERPOOL. HE IS AN AMAZING PLAYER."

THIERRY HENRY

MARCH 4, 2006 FULHAM 0—4 ARSENAL
(HENRY 31, 77, ADEBAYOR 35, FABREGAS 86)
MARCH 12, 2006 ARSENAL 2—1 LIVERPOOL
(HENRY 21, 84)
MARCH 18, 2006 ARSENAL 3—0 CHARLTON ATHLETIC
(PIRES 13, ADEBAYOR 32, HLEB 49)

MARCH 2006

Three matches, three wins, nine goals. What a great month for Arsène Wenger's men.

An exceptionally satisfying month for Arsenal began with a trip to West London to take on Fulham at Craven Cottage. Within 35 minutes, the Gunners were 2–0 ahead after Thierry Henry and Adebayor both found the back of the net. Henry got his second and Arsenal's third in the 77th minute. Fulham could not cope with Arsenal's confident, fluent play and, with five minutes left, Mathieu Flamini cut back for Cesc Fabregas to complete the victory.

Liverpool came to town and for much of the match, Arsenal were in complete control after going ahead in the 21st minute with a goal from Henry. After 75 minutes, Liverpool grabbed a surprise equaliser with a Luis Garcia header. Soon after this, Liverpool were reduced to ten men and then a Steven Gerrard backpass was seized upon by a rampant Henry to score a much-deserved winner.

After two great victories, Arsenal completed a March hat-trick of wins by beating Charlton Athletic 3–0 at Highbury. Robert Pires sidefooted the opening goal in

the 13th minute and it was unlucky for Charlton that they faced such an on-form Arsenal side. Adebayor had threatened to score on two occasions before finally hitting the back of the net just after the half hour mark. The win was complete four minutes after the break when Alexander Hleb smashed home a great goal.

"I FEEL THIS TEAM IS SLOWLY DISCOVERING ITS POTENTIAL, AS WELL AS IMPROVING ITS BELIEF AND ITS CONFIDENCE. YOU COULD SEE THAT AGAINST LIVERPOOL."

ARSENE WENGER

APRIL 2006

Another up and down month for the Gunners saw them collect eight points from their five matches. A draw with Spurs meant the race for a fourth-place finish with their neighbours was still on.

On April 1, Arsenal were anything other than fools as they stuck five goals past a stunned Aston Villa. A sparkling display was memorable for so many fine goals – especially Thierry Henry's brace, which comprised a fine control and chip and a curling finish after half-time. Robin Van Persie and Emmanuel Adebayor also scored and, ten minutes from time, Abou Diaby claimed his first goal for the Club.

APRIL 1, 2006 ARSENAL 5–0 ASTON VILLA
(ADEBAYOR 19, HENRY 25, 46, VAN PERSIE 71, DIABY 80)
APRIL 9, 2006 MANCHESTER UNITED 2–0 ARSENAL
APRIL 12, 2006 PORTSMOUTH 1–1 ARSENAL
(HENRY 36)
APRIL 15, 2006 ARSENAL 3–1 WEST BROMWICH ALBION
(HLEB 44, PIRES 76, BERGKAMP 89)
APRIL 22, 2006 ARSENAL 1–1 TOTTENHAM HOTSPUR
(HENRY 84)

The visit to Old Trafford was less enjoyable. Despite Henry being rested, the Gunners still started the game in fine style. However, the longer the match went on, the more the home side took control and they scored twice without reply in the second half.

In the 36th minute at Portsmouth, Henry curled in a fantastic shot from distance. But Arsenal could not convert many easier chances and left with just one point after Lua Lua's second-half equaliser.

The visit of West Brom saw Highbury turn orange for Dennis Bergkamp Day – and the Iceman himself put the icing on the cake when he set up Arsenal's second goal and scored the third himself. Before he arrived as a substitute, Alexander Hleb had given Arsenal a deserved lead. Then Bergkamp set up Robert Pires for the second and curled home the third in style.

> **DENNIS HAS INTELLIGENCE AND CLASS. CLASS IS, OF COURSE, MOST OF THE TIME LINKED TO WHAT YOU CAN DO WITH THE BALL, BUT THE INTELLIGENCE MAKES YOU USE THE TECHNIQUE IN AN EFFICIENT WAY.**
>
> **ARSENE WENGER**

If Highbury had turned orange against West Brom, then many at the ground saw red when Tottenham's captain, Robbie Keane, scored a controversial opener in the North London derby. With Champions League qualification at stake, feelings ran high and Thierry Henry's equaliser six minutes from time was, therefore, celebrated in style.

MAY 2006

A dramatic month for the Gunners saw three wins, ten goals, securing fourth place in the Premiership and, oh yes, we said goodbye to Highbury.

The Gunners kicked off the final month of the campaign by heaping pressure on rivals Tottenham Hotspur in the race for fourth place with a resounding victory over Sunderland. After laying siege on their opponents' goal, Arsenal took the lead in the 29th minute through an own goal by Danny Collins. It was no less than the Gunners deserved and their lead was doubled after 40 minutes when the great Cesc Fabregas slotted home after a clever Pires pass. Three minutes later, Henry curled home a classy free-kick to complete the victory before half-time.

The race for the precious fourth place was taken to the final day when Arsenal beat Manchester City at the City Of Manchester Stadium three days

later. Freddie Ljungberg scored his first Premiership goal of the season on the half hour mark and Jose Antonio Reyes added two late goals to ensure victory after Manchester City had come back into the game.

The final game at Highbury was suitably dramatic. The Gunners went ahead after eight minutes through Pires, but Wigan equalised two minutes later. As news filtered through of events at Upton Park (where Spurs were playing West Ham), Wigan went ahead on 33 minutes. This time it was Arsenal's turn to level matters two minutes later when Henry scored. Two second-half goals from Henry, including a 76th-minute penalty, gave him a hat-trick. With Spurs losing and Arsenal winning, it meant fourth-place for the Gunners and a place in the Champions League for 2006/2007.

> **"I FEEL THAT WE MADE FOURTH PLACE IN A FANTASTIC MANNER BECAUSE WE SCORED TEN GOALS, AND WE HAD THREE CUP GAMES BECAUSE ALL THREE TEAMS GAVE US A VERY HARD TIME. I'M VERY PROUD FOR MY TEAM."**
>
> **ARSENE WENGER**

MAY 1, 2006 SUNDERLAND 0–3 ARSENAL
(COLLINS 29 O.G., FABREGAS 40, HENRY 43)
MAY 4, 2006 MANCHESTER CITY 1–3 ARSENAL
(LJUNGBERG 30, REYES 78, 84)
MAY 7, 2006 ARSENAL 4–2 WIGAN ATHLETIC
(PIRES 8, HENRY 35, 56, 76 PEN)

Goodbye, Highbury!

Sunday May 7 was far more than the climax of the 2005/2006 season. Sit back and enjoy the highlights of a very special afternoon in the history of the stadium and the Club.

On May 7, 2006, the last ever game was played at Highbury. Fittingly enough, it was an afternoon of drama and joy. Arsenal qualified for the Champions League with victory over Wigan and then put on a 90-minute closing ceremony to see Highbury off.

DRUMMER BOYS!

The closing ceremony kicked off with a performance by the Romford Drum and Trumpet Corps.

GUNNERS GALORE!

Legendary players from throughout Arsenal's time at Highbury were paraded on the pitch to the delight of home fans of all ages!

TRUE GIANTS!
Giant models of Tony Adams, Dennis Bergkamp, Arsène Wenger and Thierry Henry also paraded. Bet they'd be handy at set-pieces!

HE'S THE BOSS!
Arsène Wenger was honoured for his achievements at Highbury.

THIERRY THE TERRIFIC!
Captain and hat-trick hero lifted the Golden Boot!

GOING OUT WITH A BANG!
A spectacular firework display brought the ceremony to a close!

FULL-TIME!
Arsène Wenger led the supporters in counting down the final ten seconds of the Highbury countdown clock.

A ROLLERCOASTER RIDE!

Relive the minute-by-minute drama of the final day of the season at Highbury, where Arsenal faced Wigan Athletic, and at Upton Park, as West Ham entertained Spurs. To finish fourth, the Gunners needed to have a better result than Tottenham.

3.00PM
Both matches kick off.

3.08PM
Robert Pires puts Arsenal 1–0 up at Highbury! Hurrah!

3.10PM
Carl Fletcher puts West Ham 1–0 up at Upton Park! Hurrah!

3.10PM
Paul Scharner equalises for Wigan at Highbury! Boo!

3.33PM
David Thompson puts Wigan ahead! Boo!

3.35PM
Jermain Defoe levels for Spurs at Upton Park! Boo!

3.35PM
Thierry Henry makes it 2–2 at Highbury! Hurrah!

4.07PM
Paul Robinson saves Teddy Sheringham's spot-kick! Boo!

4.11PM
Henry puts Arsenal back in the lead at Highbury! Hurrah!

4.31PM
Henry gives Arsenal a 4–2 lead from the penalty-spot! Hurrah!

4.35PM
Yossi Benayoun gives West Ham a 2–1 lead at Upton Park! Hurrah!

4.45PM
Full-time! Arsenal have claimed fourth spot! HURRAH!

A rsenal is a club of many joys and wonders. Here we explore 26 of them in our amazing alphabetical appreciation of Arsenal's absolute awesomeness...

A is for Arsenal, of course, by far the greatest team the world has ever seen!

B is for Dennis Bergkamp and Liam Brady – Brilliant!

C is for Cups – Arsenal love to win 'em!

D is for Doubles – Arsenal have secured them in 1971, 1998 and 2002!

E is for the magnificent Emirates Stadium, our new home!

F is for Farewell, which we fondly said to Highbury in May!

G is for Gunnersaurus, our Great mascot!

H is for Henry, our 'Thierrific' captain!

I is for Islington, the greatest borough in football!

J is for Junior Gunners, the finest supporters club on the planet!

K is for Kolo Toure, our top-class, ever-dependable centre back, who's become a real favourite with the fans!

L is for League titles – Arsenal have won 13 of them!

M is for Millennium Stadium, where Arsenal have won the FA Cup three times!

N is for the North Bank at Highbury Stadium, home to Arsenal fans since 1913!

O is for Ooh to, Ooh to be, Ooh to be a Gooner!

P is for Pires, who spent six glorious years on the Arsenal football field.

Q is for Quick march – what opponents have to do to keep up with the mighty Gunners!

R is for Royal Arsenal, the club's original name when it was first formed in south London, way back in 1886!

S is for 60,000 – the number of fans who will fit into the Emirates Stadium!

T is for total football – is there a better sight on earth than the Arsenal team in full flight?

U is for Underground – the tube station Arsenal was renamed especially for our team!

V is for *Victoria Concordia Crescit*, Arsenal's Latin motto meaning "Victory grows out of harmony"

W is for Wenger, our wonderful manager!

X is for X-ray vision – just look at the passing abilities of Bergkamp and Fabregas!

Y is for Youth – with Senderos, Fabregas, Van Persie and Walcott our squad is full of it!

Z is for zippy players, which Arsenal has plenty of – just try and keep up with Henry, Walcott, Cole...

The UEFA Champions League campaign proved to be an exciting journey for the team and fans alike. It began with an unbeaten run for the Gunners in the group stages, which left them riding high.

GROUP STAGE

Home v FC Thun (Matchday 1) **2-1**
A late Dennis Bergkamp strike sealed victory in the opening tie of Arsenal's 2005/2006 Champions League campaign. Gilberto had given the Gunners the lead six minutes after half-time but Thun struck back two minutes later. Cue the well-timed intervention of Bergkamp to save the day.

EURO FACT: THIS WAS FC THUN'S FIRST EVER CHAMPIONS LEAGUE MATCH.

Away v Ajax (Matchday 2) **2-1**
The tense closing stages of this tie should not detract from a superb Arsenal performance. Freddie Ljungberg prodded Arsenal ahead after just 80 seconds. Robert Pires doubled the lead from the penalty-spot in the 68th minute and victory seemed assured. However, Ajax scored two minutes later and Arsenal had to work hard to retain their lead.

EURO FACT: ARSENE WENGER WAS WITHOUT SIX REGULAR FIRST-TEAM PLAYERS IN AMSTERDAM.

Away v Sparta Prague (Matchday 3) **2-0**
Arsène Wenger intended to give Thierry Henry just a 30-minute run-out in this tie, but he ended up playing nearly 90 minutes after coming on for the injured Reyes. Henry scored twice and, in the process, became the greatest goalscorer in Arsenal's history with a record-breaking 186 goals. It also maintained the team's perfect record in the Champions League.

EURO FACT: SPARTA PRAGUE GOT THE IDEA FOR THEIR BLACKCURRANT SHIRTS FROM ARSENAL IN 1906.

SEPTEMBER 14, 2005 ARSENAL 2–1 FC THUN
(GILBERTO 51, BERGKAMP 90)
SEPTEMBER 27, 2005 AJAX 1–2 ARSENAL
(LJUNGBERG 2, PIRES 69 PEN)
OCTOBER 18, 2005 SPARTA PRAGUE 0–2 ARSENAL
(HENRY 21, 74)
NOVEMBER 2, 2005 ARSENAL 3–0 SPARTA PRAGUE
(HENRY 23, VAN PERSIE 81, 86)
NOVEMBER 22, 2005 FC THUN 0–1 ARSENAL
(PIRES 88 PEN)
DECEMBER 7, 2005
ARSENAL 0–0 AJAX

Home v Sparta Prague (Matchday 4) **3-0**
Although the 3–0 scoreline and guaranteed place in the next round were both satisfying, Arsenal should have won this match by a much bigger margin. Henry opened the scoring in the first-half, curling home a fine pass from Jose Antonio Reyes. Then Robin Van Persie struck twice in the final ten minutes to secure victory. On a wet night in North London, the Gunners cleaned up.

EURO FACT: THIERRY HENRY TOOK A "MOCK PENALTY" IN FRONT OF THE SOUTH STAND DURING THIS MATCH TO COMMEMORATE HIS FLUFFED SPOT-KICK IN THE PREVIOUS GAME AT HIGHBURY.

Away v FC Thun (Matchday 5) **1-0**
FC Thun played most of this match with ten men – one of their players was sent off – but held Arsenal at bay for 88 minutes. It must have been heartbreaking for them when Pires gave Arsenal the win from the penalty-spot two minutes from time. It was a bitterly cold night but Arsenal's travelling fans could bask in the glory of finishing top in their group!

EURO FACT: THIS WIN SECURED ARSENAL'S FINEST EVER START TO A EUROPEAN CAMPAIGN.

Home v Ajax (Matchday 6) **0-0**
With the top two places already decided, Arsène Wenger fielded a young team for the last group match. Had Henry netted his penalty on the stroke of half-time, Arsenal might have maintained their 100 per cent record in Group B. However, the draw kept Arsenal unbeaten and looking great for the knockout stages.

GROUP B STANDINGS

	P	W	D	L	F	A	PTS
ARSENAL	6	5	1	0	10	2	16
AJAX	6	3	2	1	10	6	11
FC THUN	6	1	1	4	4	9	4
SPARTA PRAGUE	6	0	2	4	2	9	2

Arsenal knocked us out!

After sailing through from the group stages, Arsenal reached the choppy waters of the knockout stages. However, getting past sides as strong as Real Madrid and Juventus proved plain sailing for the Arsenal crew!

SECOND ROUND FIRST LEG
Away v Real Madrid 1-0

On one of the greatest nights in the Club's history, Arsenal silenced the Bernabeu Stadium with a magnificent display. After the Gunners had dominated the opening half, they confirmed their excellence two minutes into the second period when Henry scored a superb goal. Arsenal thoroughly deserved victory and held on to claim it. It was the first time Real Madrid had been beaten at home by an English side in Europe.

SECOND ROUND SECOND LEG
Home v Real Madrid 0-0

The doubters said that, following Arsenal's surprise victory in Spain, the superstars of Real Madrid would be stung and would gain revenge here by knocking Arsenal out. But since when have the doubters known anything? Arsenal sailed through to the quarter-finals with a professional performance.

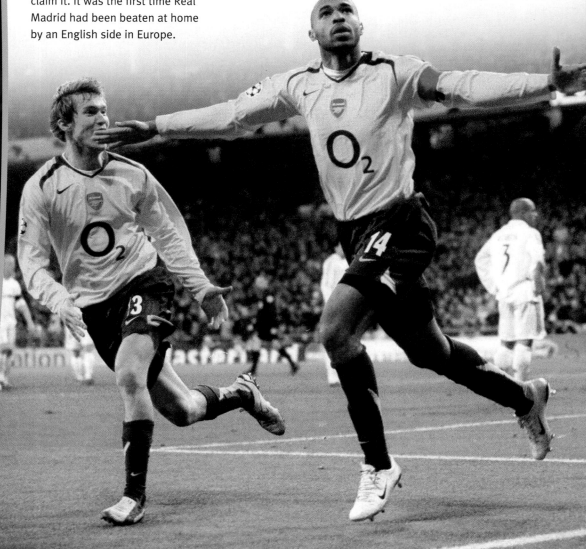

SECOND ROUND, FIRST LEG — FEBRUARY 21, 2006
REAL MADRID 0—1 ARSENAL
(HENRY 47)
SECOND LEG — MARCH 8, 2006
ARSENAL 0—0 REAL MADRID
QUARTER-FINAL, FIRST LEG — MARCH 28, 2006
ARSENAL 2—0 JUVENTUS
(FABREGAS 40, HENRY 69)
SECOND LEG — APRIL 5, 2006
JUVENTUS 0—0 ARSENAL

QUARTER-FINAL FIRST LEG
Home v Juventus 2-0

If anyone doubted Arsenal's European pedigree before this match, they surely could not have done so afterwards. The Gunners dominated their opponents – including former captain Patrick Vieira – and, in truth, should have won by a wider margin. Cesc Fabregas scored the first after 40 minutes and Henry netted against his former side in the second-half. Two Juventus players were dismissed late in the game as they chased Arsenal shadows.

QUARTER-FINAL SECOND LEG
Away v Juventus 0-0

Arsenal reached the semi-final stage of the Champions League for the first time in the Club's history at the end of a brave performance in Italy. They also got their eighth successive clean sheet in the competition, which is another record. Arsenal dominated the first-half and even when Juventus pressed more after the interval, the Gunners shut them out and sailed into the last four.

We reigned in Spain!

Spain is where two previous Arsenal Champions League campaigns came to an untimely end. But not this season! This time, the Gunners swept aside Villarreal to reach the Final. Squirrels, saves and skillful football – the Gunners were simply superb!

SEMI-FINAL FIRST LEG
Home v Villarreal 1-0

With a place in the Final of the Champions League now within sniffing distance, Arsenal nosed ahead in the first leg of a tough semi-final against Spanish side Villarreal. The Gunners were on the offensive from the start of this tie. Toure, Gilberto and Senderos all came close in the opening minutes and the home fans roared their heroes on. Shortly before half-time, the Gunners were ahead when Kolo Toure slid home Hleb's cross. One-nil to the Arsenal!

In the second-half, Arsenal had to balance their desire for a second goal with the need to deny Villarreal a chance of grabbing a vital away goal. The home team stayed on top of the play and the game finished 1-0.

EURO FACT: THIS WAS THE FINAL EUROPEAN TIE TO BE PLAYED AT HIGHBURY.

SEMI-FINAL SECOND LEG
Away v Villarreal 0-0

After so many masterful performances by Arsenal this campaign, it was probably time for one of those tense nail-biting evenings. This was one such game. In truth, the Gunners were far from their best on the night, but they kept the clean-sheet that guaranteed their place in their first ever Champions League Final.

The most memorable moment of the night came two minutes from time when Villarreal were awarded a penalty following

Clichy's challenge on Jose Mari. Jens Lehmann was not about to let the tie go into extra-time and magnificently saved Riquelme's spot-kick. Minutes later, the final whistle was blown, sparking wild celebrations on the pitch, in the stands and in homes and pubs across Britain. Arsenal reigned in Spain and had a place in the Final of the Champions League. Oh, yes!

EURO FACT: THIS WAS ARSENAL'S TENTH CONSECUTIVE CLEAN SHEET IN THE CHAMPIONS LEAGUE — A EUROPEAN RECORD.

Brave Hearts

SEMI-FINAL, FIRST LEG — APRIL 19, 2006
ARSENAL 1-0 VILLARREAL
(TOURE 41)
SECOND LEG — APRIL 25, 2006
VILLARREAL 0-0 ARSENAL

FINAL — MAY 17, 2006
ARSENAL 1—2 BARCELONA
(CAMPBELL 37)

In the Club's first ever Champions League Final, Arsenal put on a performance they, their management and fans could be truly proud of. Even playing with only ten men for much of the game, they came within a whisker of winning. Here we take a look back at an historic and proud night for Arsenal Football Club.

The Match

For days, the streets of Paris had filled with Arsenal fans, who had travelled to the French capital in the hope of seeing their favourite Parisian, Thierry Henry, lift the European Cup. Excitement filled the air.

As kick-off approached, the Stade de France filled with thousands of Gunners and Barcelona fans, who cheered their heroes onto the pitch. Arsenal started the stronger and Henry quickly received a fine pass from Emmanuel Eboue.

He shot from six yards out but saw his effort thwarted by the Barcelona goalkeeper. From the resulting corner, the captain fired in an effort from 18 yards, but was again unsuccessful.

In the 18th minute, Jens Lehmann was sent off after bringing down Eto'o outside the box. The Gunners had already been underdogs in many people's eyes – now the underdogs were down to ten men. Did the Arsenal players roll over and die? Not a bit of it! They continued to play heroically and went ahead in the 37th minute when Campbell powered home a header from a free-kick.

Cue pandemonium among the travelling fans and in Gunners-friendly homes across the world. The committed Arsenal heroes continued to fight and scrap to protect their lead deep into the second-half. Not that it was a purely rearguard action: Alexander Hleb, Freddie Ljungberg and Henry all had good chances to score.

As Arsenal fans began to glance nervously at their watches, Barcelona equalised through Eto'o. Then, four minutes later, Belletti made it two for the La Liga champions. Try as they might, Arsenal could not get back into the match as the heavens opened over Paris. Barcelona had rained on our parade.

At the final whistle there were tears, regrets and heartbreak for Gunners fans everywhere. However, there was also enormous pride. The way the young Arsenal team marched to the Final of this competition was truly awesome. Their performance on the night may not have resulted in victory, but it suggested strongly that the team could easily go one better next season.

Bravo, Gunners!

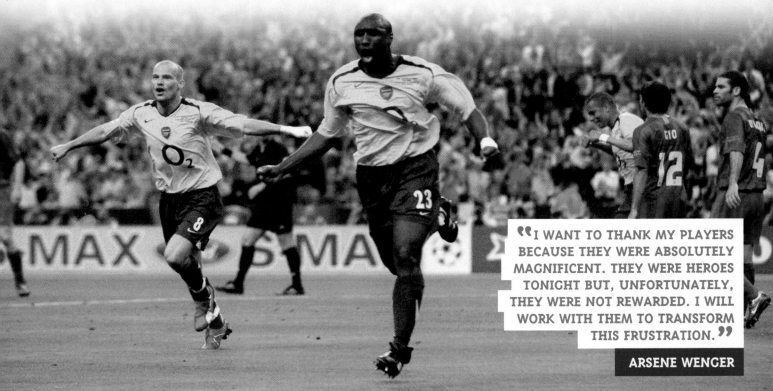

> **I WANT TO THANK MY PLAYERS BECAUSE THEY WERE ABSOLUTELY MAGNIFICENT. THEY WERE HEROES TONIGHT BUT, UNFORTUNATELY, THEY WERE NOT REWARDED. I WILL WORK WITH THEM TO TRANSFORM THIS FRUSTRATION.**
>
> **ARSENE WENGER**

Thierry's Terrific Times!

Gunners captain Thierry Henry became Arsenal's all-time record goalscorer during the 2005/2006 season. He netted his 186th Gunners goal against Sparta Prague and eclipsed the record set by Ian Wright. Here, we've selected five fantastic strikes from Thierry's Arsenal career for you to enjoy looking back over.

ARSENAL 4–2 LIVERPOOL
April 9, 2004

In the previous week, the Gunners had been knocked out of the FA Cup and Champions League and were behind at half-time against Liverpool. Were they going to lose out in the League too? Not when Thierry is around! He scored a breathtaking individual goal and went on to score a hat-trick.

ARSENAL 1–0 MAN UNITED
October 1, 2000

Thierry had a pretty terrific record against Manchester United but this was probably his best goal against them. Receiving the ball on the corner of the area he twisted round and fired it into the top corner of the net. Like many great Thierry goals, it was as if the defence and goalkeeper were not there!

SOUTHAMPTON 0–1 ARSENAL
September 18, 1999

This was Thierry's first strike for the Club in his ninth Arsenal game. He collected a fine pass from then captain Tony Adams and curled home the winning goal into the far corner. Who would have thought then how many more goals he would go on to score for Arsenal?

ARSENAL 3–2 ASTON VILLA
December 9, 2001

Having gone 2–0 down in this match, victory seemed unlikely to say the least. However, once the scoreline was level anything was possible. Cometh the final minute, cometh the man and Thierry raced through to score the winning goal.

ARSENAL 3–0 TOTTENHAM HOTSPUR
November 16, 2002

Thierry raced from one penalty area to the other, beating four Tottenham players on the way. He turned into the box from his right and then slammed a left-footed shot past Kasey Keller. Having run the length of the pitch to score, he did the same to celebrate!

> **I ALWAYS REFER TO ARSENAL AS MY HOME. I HAVE BEEN WELCOMED WITH OPEN ARMS, THE LOVE I RECEIVE HERE ... IS SOMETHING I CAN'T FORGET ABOUT.**
>
> THIERRY HENRY

GOALS PER SEASON

Season	Prem	Europe	FAC	FLC	Other	Total
1999/2000	17	8	0	1	0	26
2000/2001	17	4	1	0	0	22
2001/2002	24	7	1	0	0	32
2002/2003	24	7	1	0	0	32
2003/2004	30	5	3	0	1	39
2004/2005	25	5	0	0	0	30
2005/2006	26	5	0	1	0	32
TOTALS	**163**	**41**	**6**	**2**	**1**	**213**

All Premiership home matches and selected home cup ties, during the 2005/2006 season, were given themes to help celebrate Arsenal's 93-year stay at Highbury. There were also many other nods to the Stadium's past during the campaign. Here we look back at some of the highlights of Highbury's farewell events...

MANY HAPPY RETURNS!

The home game against Manchester City was made Arsène Wenger Day. It was an appropriate choice as it was the manager's birthday. Supporters sang "Happy Birthday" to the Frenchman before the game.

DENNIS' DUTCH DELIGHT!

For the visit of West Bromwich Albion, Highbury turned orange as supporters celebrated the Dutch master himself, Dennis Bergkamp. Supporters from Ajax also attended and special orange t-shirts were handed out to fans. Dennis marked the occasion by coming off the bench with the scores at 1–1, setting up the goal that made it 2–1 and scoring the one that made it 3–1!

SCORES ON THE DOORS!

The Club resurrected a number of Highbury traditions during the campaign, none more fun than the reappearance of the old half-time scoreboard. Before these days of Jumbotron screens and technology, the half-time scores around the country were displayed manually. It was fun to see how things used to be done but we'll stick with the hi-tech stuff from now on!

EUROPEAN NIGHTS!

The match against FC Thun was designated European Nights Day and who better to mark it than Alan Smith, who scored the winning goal for Arsenal in the 1994 European Cup Winners' Cup Final against Parma? That said, there were some pretty special European nights during the 2005/2006 season!

BACK FOUR DAY

The home match against Man United was awarded the theme of Back Four Day. The fans were thrilled to welcome back Lee Dixon, Martin Keown and Nigel Winterburn to help mark this special day. The current back four kept a clean sheet during the match, which ended 0–0.

LET'S CELEBRATE!

The Fulham match was Goal Celebrations Day. Christopher Wreh – who celebrated the goals he scored during Arsenal's 1997/1998 Double season with spectacular somersaults – returned and met up with current striking hero Thierry Henry.

GREAT SAVES DAY

Before the home match against Chelsea, Arsenal goalkeeping legends David Seaman and Bob Wilson returned to the pitch to discuss their greatest moments in an Arsenal shirt.

THE FIN

AL SALUTE

Our New Home!

The waiting is over and the Emirates Stadium is finally open for business – the business of football! Here's a look at just a few of the features that will make life at the Emirates a joy for players and fans alike! Hold onto your hats – this is going to be a very exciting home for us all!

UPSTAIRS DOWNSTAIRS!

There are 100 flights of stairs, the combined height of which is enough to go to the top of Canary Wharf twice over. But don't worry about your legs; there are 13 elevators and five banks of escalators to take you to the top of the stands! In addition, the stadium contains 2,000 doors.

PITCH PERFECT!

Visitors to Highbury always commented on the superb quality of the playing surface. And with the attractive style of play that Arsène Wenger has demanded from his team, a perfect pitch is even more important! At Emirates Stadium, the Club has invested in a full-scale, revolutionary pitch growth and lighting system which will help to produce perfect grass-growing conditions – even in the freezing winter months! The size of the grass area at Emirates Stadium – the pitch and surrounds – is 113m by 76m, compared to 105m by 70m at Highbury, or about 15 per cent larger.

SUPER SIGNING!

Arsenal-supporting chef, Raymond Blanc, who has won two Michelin stars, is the Chef Director for the restaurant at the Diamond Club. He and his team will provide world-class food for Arsenal fans. Another great signing by Arsenal!

FEEDING THE 60,000

Feeling peckish after reading that? There are 250 catering points around the stadium and the Club will be able to serve up to 2,000 meals to the 150 Executive Boxes on matchday. Yum!

WE'RE THE CLOCK END!

First erected in the 1930/1931 season, the Arsenal clock has become a legendary sight. A replica of this clock has been created for the Diamond Club. Half the size of the original, this clock will tell the time for Club members and ensure they are never late for kick-off!

SMART THINKING!

Season ticket books will be replaced by Smartcards at our new home. The size of a credit card, supporters will swipe the card in order to gain access to the stadium. This helps prevent forgery and touting and also means you will get into the stadium quicker than ever!

Emirates Stadium
The new home of Arsenal

What with their successful run in the Champions League and the effort required to keep in touch in an increasingly competitive Premiership, something had to give. Arsenal have dominated the FA Cup in recent years but this season they made an early exit. Here we relive 2006's FA Cup run.

THIRD ROUND
Home v Cardiff City

Victory for Arsenal was never in serious doubt here as the Gunners made a fantastic start to the FA Cup campaign. Robert Pires twice finished excellent moves with two goals in the opening 18 minutes and that laid an unbeatable foundation for Arsenal. Who would the draw pair them with for the next round?

MATCH FACT: THIS MATCH MARKED ENGLAND YOUTH INTERNATIONAL KERREA GILBERT'S FIRST-TEAM DEBUT.

FOURTH ROUND
Away v Bolton Wanderers

Oh no, not away to Bolton Wanderers! In recent years, the North-west side have often emerged on top when the Gunners have visited their ground. This proved to be the case again. Sol Campbell and Robin Van Persie both struck the woodwork but victory went to the home side and Arsenal were out of the FA Cup.

MATCH FACT: THIS WAS ONLY THE SECOND TIME THAT ARSENAL HAVE BEEN KNOCKED OUT OF THE FA CUP BEFORE THE SEMI-FINAL STAGE SINCE ARSENE WENGER TOOK OVER.

THIRD ROUND – JANUARY 7, 2006
ARSENAL 2–1 CARDIFF CITY
(PIRES 6, 18)

FOURTH ROUND – JANUARY 28, 2006
BOLTON WANDERERS 1–0 ARSENAL

CONQUERING CARDIFF

THE F.A. CUP SPONSORED BY AXA
WINNERS 2002

In 2001, the FA Cup Final – and League Cup Final and Community Shield – moved from Wembley Stadium to the Millennium Stadium in Cardiff and stayed there for six years. During those years, Arsenal played in four of the six FA Cup Finals and four of the Community Shields. The Millennium Stadium almost became the Gunners' second home! Here we relive the best matches during Arsenal's Cardiff domination!

FA CUP FINAL 2002
Arsenal 2–0 Chelsea

Half of London decamped to Cardiff for this final and the Gunners emerged on top. Two fine second-half goals from Ray Parlour and Freddie Ljungberg were enough to give victory to Arsenal at the end of this entertaining and hard-fought match.

COMMUNITY SHIELD 2002
Arsenal 1–0 Liverpool

Having won the World Cup during the summer, Brazilian Gilberto thought it might be a nice idea to add the Community Shield to his summer trophy haul. He came off the bench at half-time and, in the 68th minute, drilled home the winner.

FA CUP FINAL 2003
Arsenal 1–0 Southampton

Robert Pires had missed the 2002 FA Cup Final through injury but he made up for that disappointment by scoring the winner against Southampton. Arsenal were on top for much of the game and, thanks to Pires' 32nd-minute strike, they retained the FA Cup.

TIES TO FORGET

FA Cup Final 2001
Arsenal 1–2 Liverpool
The Gunners dominate the match and take the lead but are shot down by a brace of late Michael Owen goals.

Community Shield 2003
**Arsenal 1–1 Manchester United
(United win 4–3 on penalties)**
The game finished level after Thierry Henry cancelled out United's opener but the Gunners lost after a penalty shoot-out.

Community Shield 2005
Arsenal 1–2 Chelsea
Two Didier Drogba goals secure victory for Chelsea, despite a good performance by Arsenal, capped by a Cesc Fabregas goal.

Community Shield 2004
Arsenal 3–1 Manchester United
Jose Antonio Reyes was the star as Arsenal swept aside Manchester United with ease. He set up Gilberto's opener and claimed the second goal himself. Then a third was added by Ashley Cole. Another Cardiff victory for the Gunners!

FA Cup Semi-Final 2005
Arsenal 3–0 Blackburn Rovers
The Gunners held off a robust challenge from Blackburn to book another FA Cup Final appearance. Robert Pires scored after 42 minutes and Robin Van Persie added two more late in the second-half.

FA Cup Final 2005
**Arsenal 0–0 Manchester United
(Arsenal won 5–4 on penalties)**
Although the Gunners were, in truth, second-best for much of this tie, they still won the Cup after the first ever Final decided by a penalty shoot-out. After Jens Lehmann brilliantly saved Paul Scholes' spot-kick, it was down to Patrick Vieira to win the Cup by converting his attempt. Vieira's last kick for Arsenal won them the FA Cup!

Teenage Kicks!

Everyone knows that Arsenal's first-team is already loaded with some of the Premiership's finest, youngest stars.

Cesc Fabregas has become one of European football's hottest talents and has set a fine example for other youngsters on the Gunners' books. Add to that the form of Robin Van Persie, Emmanuel Eboue, Philippe Senderos and other youngsters during the 2005/2006 campaign and you can see that Arsenal is the place to be for youthful football talent.

Here, we profile the Young Guns who are ready to challenge for a permanent place in the first-team during the Club's inaugural season at the Emirates Stadium.

THE ENGLISH HIT-MAN
Name: Theo Walcott
Born: March 16, 1989
Position: Attacking midfielder

The lowdown: Theo, England's youngest ever international (at 17 years and 75 days), was Arsenal's third signing of the 2006 transfer window when he arrived from Championship side Southampton. He can operate as a winger or a striker and is rumoured to be even faster than Thierry Henry. Theo is assured a fantastic future with the Gunners.

THE SOLID SWISS
Name: Johan Djourou
Born: January 18, 1987
Position: Defender

The lowdown: Philippe Senderos is not the only young Swiss defender on Arsenal's books – Johan is there too! A great reader of the game and assured in possession, Johan has made some impressive first-team performances. He can also play at full back, giving him even more chances to play on the highest stage.

THE PACESETTER

Name: Justin Hoyte
Born: November 20, 1984
Position: Defender

The lowdown: Another of Arsène Wenger's exciting young English talents, Justin might have spent last season on loan at Sunderland but he has always impressed on his first-team appearances for the Gunners. He has played in the Premiership, Community Shield and Champions League for Arsenal and, with his pace and ability going forward, he is definitely one to watch!

THE SUPER SWEDE!

Name: Sebastian Larsson
Born: June 6, 1985
Position: Midfielder

The lowdown: Sebastian decided not to go out on loan for the 2005/2006 season and his decision to stay was vindicated when he made appearances in all four competitions this campaign. He set up and scored goals during the Carling Cup campaign and played a full 90-minute match in the Champions League. A fine passer and dead-ball specialist, Sebastian is set for more action.

THE ITALIAN JOB

Name: Arturo Lupoli
Born: June 24, 1987
Position: Striker

The lowdown: Arturo is one of the Reserve League's most prolific goalscorers. He's scored for the first-team in successive seasons during Carling Cup ties, against Everton and Reading. He was born in Brescia in Italy and played for Parma before signing for the Gunners in July 2004.

THE ENGLISH ROCK

Name: Kerrea Gilbert
Born: February 28, 1987
Position: Defender

The lowdown: Kerrea has many fans and Thierry Henry is one of them. The captain praised the form of Kerrea (pronounced Kerry) after the England youth international's cross set up his goal in the semi-final against Wigan. The athletic, pacey youngster has also impressed in the FA Cup and looks set for a fine future at Arsenal.

"They are very young and very strong," so said Arsène Wenger when asked about the players who formed the Arsenal team for another useful run in the Carling Cup. Here we look back at the games that saw the young Gunners once more give the fans a glimpse into the future...

THIRD ROUND
Away v Sunderland

Sunderland's offer of reduced-price tickets for this tie meant a sell-out crowd produced a typically passionate north-east atmosphere for Arsenal's opening match in the Carling Cup. A blend of youngsters (including Emmanuel Eboue and Sebastian Larsson), some more experienced players (Sol Campbell and Pascal Cygan) and one debutant (Fabrice Muamba) gelled in style and secured a comprehensive victory.

Just past the hour mark, Eboue received the ball 30 yards from goal and fired an unstoppable shot into the top corner to give Arsenal a deserved lead. Six minutes later, Arturo Lupoli was fouled in the area and Robin Van Persie walloped the resultant penalty home to double the visitors' lead. Then, with just three minutes left, Larsson fed Van Persie, who slotted the ball past the advancing goalkeeper to tie up a fantastic win for Arsène Wenger's men.

FOURTH ROUND
Home v Reading

Arsène Wenger's young guns sailed into the last eight of the Carling Cup with a convincing win over Reading at Highbury. The most experienced Arsenal player on the pitch was Jose Antonio Reyes and the least experienced was Kerrea Gilbert making his full first-team debut. Meanwhile, Reading fielded three former Gunners – Graham Stack, James Harper and Steven Sidwell.

In the 12th minute, Quincy Owusu-Abeyie fed Reyes, who drew the visiting goalkeeper and tucked the ball home. Three minutes before half-time, Reyes turned provider when he passed to Robin Van Persie on the edge of the area. The Dutchman fired the ball home. In the 65th minute, substitute Arturo Lupoli took the ball round the advancing Stack and made it 3–0, thus confirming beyond doubt Arsenal's place in the quarter-finals.

THIRD ROUND – OCTOBER 25, 2005
SUNDERLAND 0–3 ARSENAL
(EBOUE 61, VAN PERSIE 67 PEN, 87)
FOURTH ROUND – NOVEMBER 29, 2005
ARSENAL 3–0 READING
(REYES 12, VAN PERSIE 42, LUPOLI 65)
QUARTER-FINAL – DECEMBER 21, 2005
DONCASTER ROVERS 2–2 ARSENAL (ARSENAL 3–1 PENS)
(OWUSU-ABEYIE 63, GILBERTO 120)

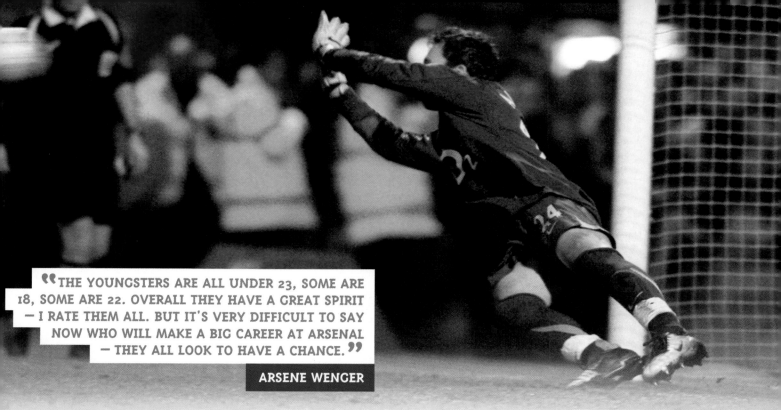

> **"THE YOUNGSTERS ARE ALL UNDER 23, SOME ARE 18, SOME ARE 22. OVERALL THEY HAVE A GREAT SPIRIT — I RATE THEM ALL. BUT IT'S VERY DIFFICULT TO SAY NOW WHO WILL MAKE A BIG CAREER AT ARSENAL — THEY ALL LOOK TO HAVE A CHANCE."**
>
> **ARSENE WENGER**

QUARTER-FINAL
Away v Doncaster Rovers

An incredible and dramatic evening of football ended with Arsenal celebrating victory in a penalty shoot-out and a place in the Carling Cup semi-final. It was all-square after 90 minutes, but the Gunners looked to be on their way out when Doncaster Rovers scored in extra-time. However, there were to be more twists in this tale.

Quincy Owusu-Abeyie scored Arsenal's first on the night, a deflected 63rd-minute effort that cancelled out Michael McIndoe's fourth-minute opener. When Doncaster regained the lead through substitute Paul Green in extra-time, it looked to be curtains for the Gunners. However, in the 120th minute, Gilberto tumbled in the area but managed to hook the ball home as he did so.

So to the penalty shoot-out. Gilberto, Pascal Cygan and Sebastian Larsson all scored, but Alexander Hleb's potential winning kick was saved. This allowed Manuel Almunia, who saved the next Doncaster penalty, to spark the wild celebrations. The young Gunners were two games from the final. Could they go all the way?

SEMI-FINAL FIRST LEG
Away v Wigan Athletic

After an Arsenal-dominated first-half and a 12-minute delay due to power failure, Wigan grabbed a vital lead to end the first leg of the semi-final on top. Paul Scharner is a Gunners fan but on his debut for Wigan he scored against his heroes.

Freddie Ljungberg, Mathieu Flamini and Gilberto all had chances to score but were unable to find the back of the net during this edgy cup tie. However, in the 77th minute, Scharner capitalised on his chance to give Wigan the advantage for the second leg at Highbury.

SEMI-FINAL SECOND LEG
Home v Wigan Athletic

Until the 119th minute of this remarkable tie, Arsenal fans believed that their side would prevail and reach their first League Cup Final for 13 years. Then, Jason Roberts broke their hearts.

> **"YES, I WAS DISAPPOINTED WITH THE WAY WE CONCEDED THE GOAL. IT WAS ONE MINUTE TO GO, GOAL KICK TO US AND WE ARE OUT OF THE COMPETITION."**
>
> **ARSENE WENGER**

Wenger rolled out some bigger names for this tie and Thierry Henry opened the scoring in the 65th minute with a close-range header. Then, three minutes into the second period of extra-time, Robin Van Persie sent home a fine free-kick. Earlier in the match, Jose Antonio Reyes had missed a penalty; the Gunners were dominating the goals and the chances.

However, with 65 seconds left, Jason Roberts capitalised on confusion in the Arsenal defence to equalise the aggregate score and send Wigan to the final on the away goals rule.

SEMI-FINAL, 1ST LEG — JANUARY 10, 2006
WIGAN ATHLETIC 1-0 ARSENAL

SEMI-FINAL, 2ND LEG — JANUARY 24, 2006
ARSENAL 2-1 WIGAN ATHLETIC
(HENRY 65, VAN PERSIE 108)

The Arsenal players work hard in training to make sure they stay at the top of their game. If you want to become a star at Arsenal then you too need to train like a champion. Here are some basic tips to get you going...

DO!

- Warm-up and stretch before every session.

- Make sure you practice with your weaker foot as well as your stronger one.

- Incorporate rest days into your schedule.

- Refuel sensibly – that means eating as healthily as possible and drinking plenty of water.

- Practice sprints over short distances to improve your speed on the pitch.

DON'T!

- Concentrate on developing just your upper or lower body – you need to be balanced!

- Overdo it – even world champions need to rest!

- Take it too seriously – football is a game and should always be fun!

- Bend the rules – cheats never prosper!

- Concentrate on being good in one position only – if you are adaptable you will have an edge on your rivals.

- Think you know it all – listen and learn from your coaches.

In a campaign of wonder goals, historic goals and significant strikes, these are the ten greatest goals we've had the pleasure of witnessing this season!

10

Scorer: Robin Van Persie
Match: Arsenal 2–0 Newcastle, August 14, Premiership
The goal: Fans were starting to think that Given couldn't be beaten in Arsenal's first home game, but six minutes after Henry's 81st-minute penalty, Robin Van Persie popped up with a fine precision shot to beat the keeper at the near post.

9

Scorer: Thierry Henry
Match: Arsenal 2–1 Liverpool, March 12, Premiership
The goal: One of many goals where Thierry combined with Cesc Fabregas, this one saw the Frenchman sprint forward and clip a fine goal past the visiting goalkeeper. Get in!

8

Scorer: Jose Antonio Reyes
Match: Man City 1–3 Arsenal, May 4, Premiership
The goal: Jose came off the bench to score twice in this tie but it was his second that caught the eye. He received the ball from Thierry and curled an exquisite shot into the top corner of the net.

7

Scorer: Dennis Bergkamp
Match: Arsenal 3–1 West Brom, April 15, Premiership
The goal: Well, it was Dennis Bergkamp Day at Highbury so the Dutchman was destined to score. A second-half substitute, Dennis received the ball and curled it home with characteristic style and class.

6

Scorer: Kolo Toure
Match: Arsenal 1–0 Villarreal, April 19, Champions League
The goal: Although this goal was tapped home from close range, it is included for its significance. This goal sent Arsenal to their first ever Champions League Final. This was an historic goal.

5

Scorer: Thierry Henry
Match: Real Madrid 0–1 Arsenal, February 21, Champions League
The goal: Henry picked up the ball in the centre circle, beat three Real players, including Ronaldo, before reaching the penalty area and slotted the ball past Casillas into the far corner of the net. Really good!

4

Scorer: Robin Van Persie
Match: Arsenal 3–0 Blackburn Rovers, November 26, Premiership
The goal: In the final minute, Robin ghosted between two defenders and scored from an almost impossible angle. However many times you watch this goal you still cannot work out how he did it.

3

Scorer: Thierry Henry
Match: Arsenal 1–1 Spurs, April 22, Premiership
The goal: With just seven minutes of the game remaining, and Champions League qualification in jeopardy, the captain took the ball and flicked it into the far corner. And what a celebration!

2

Scorer: Thierry Henry
Match: Arsenal 4–2 Wigan Athletic, May 7, Premiership
The goal: Yes, another Thierry goal, even if it was a penalty! But it was the final goal to be scored at Highbury, the final goal of his hat-trick and the goal that confirmed Arsenal's Champions League qualification. No wonder Thierry kissed the hallowed turf!

1

Scorer: Cesc Fabregas
Match: Arsenal 2–0 Juventus, March 28, Champions League
The goal: Robert Pires robs Patrick Vieira and passes to Thierry Henry, who feeds Cesc Fabregas. The young Spaniard cushions the ball, slots it home and Highbury erupts with joy. Some goals are unforgettable.

A player's number is now a huge part of his identity on the pitch. But who wore those same numbers in the past for Arsenal? And why do certain numbers have special significance for players? The answers are here in a maths lesson you won't want to miss...

1

Now: Jens Lehmann
Then: David Seaman – David played for Arsenal between 1990 and 2003. He won three league titles, three FA Cups, a League Cup and a European Cup Winners' Cup. He was also a regular for the England team.
Then: Bob Wilson – The man they call "Willow" kept goal for Arsenal and was the Gunners' Player of the Season when the team won the double in the 1970–71 season. He has since become a broadcasting legend and formed a charity, The Willow Foundation, that improves the lives of seriously ill young adults.

3

Now: Ashley Cole
Then: Nigel Winterburn – Nigel joined Arsenal in 1987 and went on to win three league titles, two FA Cups, a League Cup and a European Cup Winners' Cup.
Then: Kenny Sansom – Kenny was a legendary left-back for club and country. He remains England's most-capped full-back. He played in two World Cup Finals for England and won the League Cup with Arsenal in 1987. He is now one of the "Three Wise Men" in the Arsenal magazine.

8

Now: Freddie Ljungberg
Then: Ian Wright – Ian was a goalscoring legend for Arsenal in the 1990s. Arsenal's second highest goalscorer, Wright was a key part of the 1998 double-winning team and won other trophies, including a League Cup, two FA Cups and a European Cup Winners' Cup. Wright, awarded an MBE in 2002, also starred for England.

Now: Jose Antonio Reyes

Then: Nicolas Anelka – Nicolas was an unknown youngster when Arsène Wenger plucked him from Paris St Germain, but he went on to star in Arsenal's 1998 double-winning side.

Now: Robin Van Persie

Then: Marc Overmars – Like Van Persie, Overmars was a Dutchman who scared the life out of opposition defenders. However, Overmars – who starred in the 1998 double season and scored the winning goal at Old Trafford that year – operated on the wing.

Now: Emmanuel Adebayor

Then: Nwankwo Kanu – Nwankwo was Emmanuel's hero and Emmanuel chose the 25 shirt in tribute to him. Kanu was a similar player in many ways to Emmanuel and his cheeky tricks enlivened many a game during his stay at the Club at the turn of the century.

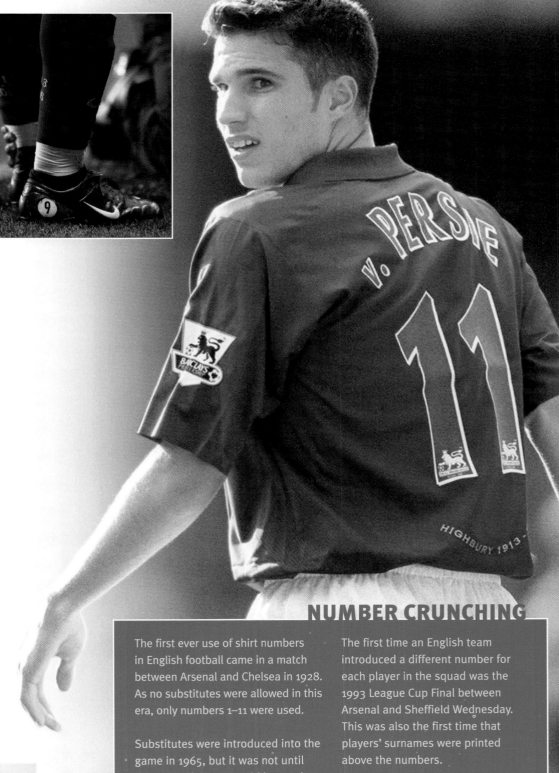

NUMBER CRUNCHING

The first ever use of shirt numbers in English football came in a match between Arsenal and Chelsea in 1928. As no substitutes were allowed in this era, only numbers 1–11 were used.

Substitutes were introduced into the game in 1965, but it was not until the 1980s that two could be used in English football. Most subs wore either 12 or 14, because many players were superstitious and didn't want to wear number 13. Three subs came in during the 1990s.

The first time an English team introduced a different number for each player in the squad was the 1993 League Cup Final between Arsenal and Sheffield Wednesday. This was also the first time that players' surnames were printed above the numbers.

Many players, in a number of sports, have chosen the squad number 23, including Sol Campbell. This is often in tribute to basketball legend Michael Jordan, who wore that number.

The Dream XI

Like all dinosaurs, Gunnersaurus has been around for quite a while. So who better to name an all-time Arsenal Eleven? Here, the mascot grants a rare audience and names his Arsenal Dream Team. He reckons this team would win every trophy going. But who has made the final line-up?

Goalkeeper: Bob Wilson
"Before he became a TV star, Bob was a star between the sticks for the Gunners. He was player of the season for the Club's 1970/1971 double-winning season. He also does great work for charity through the Willow Foundation. Top man!"

Right-back: Lee Dixon
"Part of the famous five that kept clean sheet after clean sheet as Arsenal won four league titles between 1989 and 2002, Dixon was a solid, reliable defender. You might catch him on the BBC nowadays!"

Left-back: Kenny Sansom
"A solid player for Arsenal and England, Kenny was also the captain of the Gunners for many years in the 1980s. He was quick, reliable and could fire in a handy cross. He played 394 games for the Gunners."

Centre-back: Kolo Toure
"What's not to like about Kolo? He is enthusiastic, committed, solid and a mighty nice guy too! And he scored the goal that meant Arsenal reached their first ever Champions League Final. You're cool, Kolo!"

Centre-back: Tony Adams
"'There's only one Tony Adams', the fans would chant and they are right. The captain during some of Arsenal's most successful years, Tony steered the club to trophies galore! He was also the first player to win the league championship in three different decades."

Right Midfield: David Rocastle

"Rocky was an Arsenal hero who won a League Cup and two league titles with the Club in the 1980s and 1990s. He died in 2001 at the age of just 33. See page 51 for details of the charity in his memory."

Left Midfield: Marc Overmars

"Marc absolutely flew down the wing for Arsenal and was a key player for the team in the 1997–98 double-winning season. The flying Dutchman, indeed!"

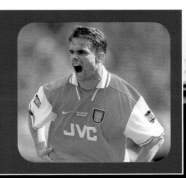

Central Midfield: Liam Brady

"Liam was a fantastic midfielder. He was known as 'Chippy', less for his chipped goals than for his love of chip suppers. I can't blame him; I enjoy them myself! He is now Arsenal's Head of Youth Development."

Central Midfield: Patrick Vieira

"Who can forget Patrick? A midfield powerhouse, a successful Arsenal captain and an all-round nice guy: we were all sad when he moved on, but he left behind some fantastic memories for all Gooners!"

Centre Forward: Thierry Henry

"Like all Gooners, I am off my seat every time Thierry starts whizzing towards goal with the ball at his feet. The Club's record goalscorer, Thierry will be an Arsenal legend for ever and ever."

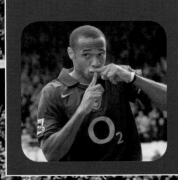

Centre Forward: Ian Wright

"'Ian Wright, Wright Wright! Ian Wright, Wright, Wright!' How I used to love chanting that. Wrighty was a goalscoring legend who won every domestic honour there is to win with Arsenal."

Joint coaches: Herbert Chapman and Arsène Wenger

"I can't choose between these two for the coaching role so they would have to share the dug-out. Arsenal won — among other things — their first league title under Herbert in 1930, also winning three in a row. But the Gunners have won trophies galore under Arsène too."

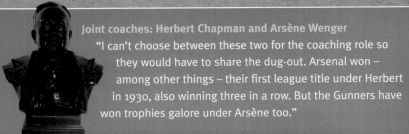

Junior Gunners

It has been another vintage year for the greatest supporters club on the planet. Gunnersaurus talks you through just some of the highlights.

QUESTION TIME!

In February 2006, Cesc Fabregas and Johan Djourou were quizzed by 45 lucky Junior Gunners at the first Junior Gunners Forum! Arsenal vice-chairman David Dein also came along to chair the event. The players answered a range of questions, including which player has the worst fashion sense at the Club (Freddie Ljungberg according to Cesc!) and which player they would most like to bring to the Club (Johan said he'd love to bring back Patrick Vieira). Afterwards, all those Junior Gunners present received signed photos of Cesc and Johan. More Junior Gunners Forums are planned for the future!

TRUE CLASS

The Junior Gunners ran a fantastic competition asking members to send in projects on the history of Arsenal Stadium. Lots of excellent entries flooded in, and the winner was seven-year-old Michael Philona from Essex. His prize? He got to bring all of his school along to the home match against West Ham United!

A GLASS ACT

Junior Gunner Luke Patel presented Arsène Wenger with a set of glasses to celebrate his birthday in October 2005. Other members also helped to mark the 2,000th first-team match at Highbury (against West Ham) by unveiling a special banner before the kick-off.

MEMBERSHIP BENEFITS
There are so many reasons to join the Junior Gunners. Here are just a few:

- You could be selected to watch the first-team train on the annual members' day
- You might be photographed with the entire first-team squad at the annual photo-call
- To go on Junior Gunners trips
- To enter exclusive competitions

See the Junior Gunners section on www.arsenal.com for full details!

Charity Events

Arsenal has always supported charities and it raised £200,000 for ChildLine during the charity's two-year association with the Club. Arsenal's charity for the 2005–06 season was The David Rocastle Trust. Read on to find out how the Club raised funds for the Trust.

THE TRUST

The David Rocastle Trust remembers the Arsenal legend – nicknamed Rocky – who lost his battle with cancer in 2001 at the age of just 33. Rocky joined the Club as a 16-year-old in 1983 and won two league titles and one League Cup at Arsenal. He also won the hearts of the Arsenal faithful. The Trust was established to assist David's family, support community projects in Rocky's name and assist its beneficiaries, Great Ormond Street Hospital Children's Charity and Cancer Research UK.

ROCASTLE DAY

Arsenal's home game against Aston Villa was dedicated to David Rocastle. The game was on April 1, one day after the fifth anniversary of David's death. A number of fundraising initiatives took place, including a hospitality raffle and Junior Gunners events. Fifty pence from every match-day programme sold went to the Trust. A tribute book packed with comments from supporters was presented to David's family. The team put on its own tribute by thrashing Villa 5–0! Rocky would have really approved.

THEY HAD A BALL!

The Arsenal Charity Ball, held on May 8, 2006, raised more than £60,000 for The David Rocastle Trust and also The Arsenal Charitable Trust, which distributes funds to local causes, and has raised more than £2 million since its foundation in 1992. Hosted by Arsenal legend Bob Wilson and held at Highbury, the evening was attended by Rocastle's team-mates and all-time Arsenal legends.

Find out more about The David Rocastle Trust on the website, www.davidrocastletrust.org

IT'S THE FIRST HOME GAME OF THE NEW SEASON AND GUNNERSAURUS IS HAVING HIS FAVOURITE PRE-MATCH MEAL OF BAKED BEANS ON TOAST WASHED DOWN BY A MUG OF TEA (WITH TWO SUGARS).

I CAN'T WAIT FOR THE MATCH TO START. I'VE GOT A FEELING IT'S GOING TO BE OUR YEAR.

GUNNERSAURUS LEAVES THE HOUSE AND SETS OFF FOR THE STADIUM.

HAVE I GOT EVERYTHING I NEED? ARSENAL SCARF, LUCKY HANDKERCHIEF, NEW SEASON TICKET, MONEY.....

GUNNERSAURUS WALKS TOWARDS THE GROUND IN A DAYDREAM.

EBOUE TO FLAMINI TO FABREGAS TO HENRY... GOALLLL!!!!!

GUNNERSAURUS ARRIVES OUTSIDE THE PORTICOS OF THE OLD ARSENAL STADIUM, AND STOPS WITH A START.

WHERE IS EVERYBODY? IT MUST BE NEARLY TIME FOR THE KICK-OFF.

A NEWSPAPER-SELLER ON A NEAR-BY CORNER HELPS HIM OUT.

WHAT'S UP, SON? GOT A BIT LOST? IF YOU'RE LOOKING FOR THE EMIRATES STADIUM GO LEFT HERE, RIGHT AT THE NEXT CORNER, THEN LEFT AND RIGHT AGAIN. YOU CAN'T MISS IT!

THANKS, MISTER.

GUNNERSAURUS RUNS PAST THE ARSENAL TUBE STATION.

ARSENAL

I'VE GOT TO HURRY, IT'S NEARLY TIME FOR THE KICK-OFF.

GUNNERSAURUS SCAMPERS ACROSS THE PEDESTRIAN WALKWAY OVER THE RAILWAY LINE THAT LEADS TO EMIRATES STADIUM.

COR! THIS PLACE IS BIGGER THAN I THOUGHT.

GUNNERSAURUS WEAVES HIS WAY THROUGH THE CROWDS MILLING AROUND THE PERIMETER CONCOURSE OF THE STADIUM.

PANT! PANT!

GUNNERSAURUS IS INSIDE THE GROUND, ARRIVES AT THE TOP OF THE STEPS AND GETS HIS FIRST VIEW OF THE NEW STADIUM.

WELCOME TO EMIRATES STADIUM

WOW! IT'S FANTASTIC.

GUNNERSAURUS SITS BACK IN HIS SEAT, SURVEYING THE SCENE.

SAY WHAT YOU LIKE, THERE'S NO PLACE LIKE HOME!

...DON'T FORGET TO CHECK OUT THE JUNIOR GUNNERS INFORMATION ON PAGE 50!

CROSSWORD AND SPOT THE DIFFERENCE

ACROSS

1 Teenager signed from Southampton in 2006 (4, 7)
7 Thierry is a goalscoring _____ (3)
8 Lower limb (3)
9 A cup match you could wear around your neck (3)
10 Nationality of Philippe Senderos (5)
12 A flood _____ makes it easy to watch matches in the dark (5)
14 North African country, home of the Pyramids (5)
16 Work out a puzzle (5)
17 The second month in short (3)
19 Dennis Bergkamp, the _____ man (3)
20 Family pet that barks (3)
21 19____, the year Carling Cup kid Fabrice Muamba was born (6, 5)

DOWN

1 The money paid to buy a player (8, 3)
2 A good striker has a good one for goal (3)
3 British country England played in the World Cup 2006 qualifiers (5)
4 Within the laws (5)
5 The FA Cup is a knock _____ competition (3)
6 Age of Thierry Henry at the end of the 2005–06 season (6, 5)
11 When it's this, pitches can get frozen (3)
13 What Jose Antonio Reyes celebrates on international duty (3)
15 _____ and turn, what a clever ball-player can do (5)
16 Mr Bould, former star centre-half, now youth team coach (5)
18 Every crowd at Emirates Stadium will be this (3)
20 What Arsène Wenger might do to unearth a new star (3)

54

(Solution on p61)

Are you a genius Gunner?

Do you think you know your Arsenal stuff? Do you reckon you are a Gunners know-it-all? Well, here's your chance to prove it! Here are 50 questions on your favourite club: can you emerge as a champion?

HIGHBURY REMEMBERED

1 In which year did Arsenal move to Highbury: 1913, 1899, or 1932?
2 The new North Stand opened in 1991. True or false?
3 Was the original North Stand called the Laundry End or the Launderette End?
4 What was the fans' name for the South Stand?
5 Was the manager's dug-out situated in the West or East Stand of the stadium?
6 A black marble bust image of which former manager resided in the Marble Halls of the stadium: Herbert Chapman or Don Howe?
7 How many luxury boxes were there in the South Stand: 53 or 197?
8 How many Jumbotron screens were there at the stadium?

9 Was the Arsenal Museum located in the North or South Stand of the stadium?
10 What was the nearby London Underground station called before Herbert Chapman got it renamed?

STRIKING FACTS

11 Both Thierry Henry and Robin Van Persie scored in the opening Premiership match of 2005/2006 against Newcastle United. But which striker got the opening goal?
12 Which Gunners hitman struck the opening goal of Arsenal's 2006 Champions League campaign?
13 Which striker hit a hat-trick in the home Premiership match against Portsmouth?

14 Theo Walcott scored in his debut for the reserves against which side: Portsmouth or Tottenham Hotspur?
15 Emmanuel Adebayor scored his first Arsenal goal against Birmingham City or Aston Villa?
16 Who was the leading Arsenal goalscorer for the 2005–06 season?
17 Emmanuel Adebayor rates which former Arsenal striker as his football hero?
18 True or false: Robin Van Persie has never scored for Arsenal in the Champions League.
19 Which former Arsenal forward now plays for Blackburn Rovers?
20 Thierry Henry has never won a trophy at international level. True or false?

TRANSFER WINDOW

21　Theo Walcott signed for Arsenal from which south coast club?

22　True or false: Abou Diaby joined the Gunners from Paris St Germain.

23　Is Arsenal Freddie Ljungberg's first or second English side?

24　Emmanuel Adebayor previously played for which French side: Monaco or Marseille?

25　Which Berkshire-based team featured three Arsenal old boys when they played the Gunners in the Carling Cup during season 2005–06?

26　Which North-east team did goalkeeper Mart Poom join Arsenal from?

27　True or false: Gilberto played for three seasons at AC Milan.

28　Cesc Fabregas started his career with which European giants: Barcelona or Juventus?

29　Thierry Henry scored during the 2005–06 Champions League against his old team. Name the team.

30　True or false: England striker Michael Owen played at Arsenal for two seasons.

THE ICEMAN

31　Which team did Dennis Bergkamp join Arsenal from?

32　Against which side did Bergkamp make his debut?

33　Dennis scored his first goal against Southampton – was this during a home match or an away match?

34　During the 1997–98 season, Dennis scored a spectacular hat-trick against Leicester City. What was the final score in that game?

35　True or false: Dennis never appeared in an FA Cup Final for Arsenal.

36　Which team did Dennis begin his career with: Ajax or PSV Eindhoven?

37　How many league titles did Dennis win with Arsenal: 2 or 3?

38　True or false: Dennis never captained Arsenal.

39　Which year was Dennis voted PFA Player Of The Year: 1998 or 2002?

40　True or false: Dennis and Robin Van Persie are cousins.

THE MANAGER

41　Arsène Wenger was born in which French city: Strasbourg or Paris?

42　True or false: Wenger played for Paris St Germain.

43　Which team did Mr Wenger join Arsenal from: Monaco or Grampus Eight?

44　Which honour did Mr Wenger receive in 2003: an OBE or MBE?

45　How many league titles has Mr Wenger won at Arsenal to date?

46　Which year did Mr Wenger join Arsenal: 1996 or 1994?

47　True or false: David Platt was Mr Wenger's first purchase for Arsenal.

48　Has Mr Wenger ever managed an international side?

49　How many FA Cups has Mr Wenger won at Highbury?

50　True or false: Mr Wenger has never been named Manager Of The Year.

Answers on p61.

All the best Arsenal players have the vision to pick out a player on a crowded pitch and pass him the ball. Can you show the same vision and solve this Arsenal wordsearch? Have a go and tick the ones you can find!

U	I	E	B	O	U	E	J	F	C	I	M	W	X
J	W	N	K	N	B	O	L	A	W	W	G	I	E
E	S	O	Y	Z	U	A	E	B	S	L	O	N	C
C	O	L	E	N	M	F	T	R	N	A	A	G	E
A	L	J	E	I	F	C	O	E	H	T	L	E	P
P	E	N	N	L	A	W	U	G	K	L	B	R	O
N	B	I	L	S	O	N	R	A	G	M	E	L	R
W	S	O	R	E	D	N	E	S	A	N	N	B	U
R	O	B	I	N	V	A	N	P	E	R	S	I	E
Y	I	E	J	L	Q	V	X	L	L	P	N	E	I
L	E	H	M	A	N	N	Y	E	P	R	E	D	N
H	J	J	L	N	I	U	I	E	K	O	L	O	M
G	U	N	N	E	R	S	H	N	N	E	T	H	H
J	J	N	W	E	N	G	E	R	J	P	E	L	X

- AFC
- COLE
- EBOUE
- EUROPE
- FABREGAS
- FLAMINI
- GAEL
- GOAL
- GUNNERS
- KOLO
- LEHMANN
- NET
- ROBIN VAN PERSIE
- SENDEROS
- SOL
- THEO
- TOURE
- WENGER
- WINGER

A

D

C

B

Chart of the matter!

It was another fantastic season for Arsenal in 2005/2006. But can The Gunners top it in 2006/2007? Keep track of everything here and compare the two campaigns!

FA PREMIERSHIP	SEASON 2005/2006	SEASON 2006/2007
Final position	Fourth	
First home win	Newcastle 2–0	
First away win	Wigan 3–2	
First home draw	Manchester Utd 0–0	
First away draw	West Ham 0–0	
First home defeat	Bolton 0–2	
First away defeat	Chelsea 0–1	

DOMESTIC CUPS	SEASON 2005/2006	SEASON 2006/2007
FA Cup	Round Four: Bolton 0–1	
Carling Cup	Semi-Final Wigan 2–2	
Community Shield	Lost to Chelsea 1–2	

CHAMPIONS LEAGUE	SEASON 2005/2006	SEASON 2006/2007
Progress	Final: Barcelona 0–1	
First home win	FC Thun 2–1	
First away win	Ajax 2–1	
First home draw	Ajax 0–0	
First away draw	Juventus 0–0	
First home defeat	None	
First away defeat	None	

GOALS	SEASON 2005/2006	SEASON 2006/2007
First in Premiership	Thierry Henry v Newcastle	
First in FA Cup	Robert Pires v Cardiff (R3)	
First in Carling Cup	Emmanuel Eboue v Sunderland (R3)	
First in Champions League	Gilberto v FC Thun	

CLEAN SHEETS	SEASON 2005/2006	SEASON 2006/2007
First in Premiership	Jens Lehmann v Newcastle	
First in FA Cup	None	
First in Carling Cup	Manuel Almunia v Sunderland	
First in Champions League	Jens Lehmann v Sparta Prague	

Answers

Spot the ball

Answer: A

Spot the difference

Here are the ten differences. Did you get them?

Arsenal Quiz

1	1913	26	Sunderland
2	False	27	False
3	The Laundry End	28	Barcelona
4	The Clock End	29	Juventus
5	East Stand	30	False
6	Herbert Chapman	31	Inter Milan
7	53	32	Middlesbrough
8	Two	33	A home match
9	North	34	3–3
10	Gillespie Road	35	False
11	Henry	36	Ajax
12	Bergkamp	37	3
13	Henry	38	False
14	Portsmouth	39	1998
15	Birmingham City	40	False
16	Henry	41	Strasbourg
17	Nwankwo Kanu	42	False
18	False	43	Grampus Eight
19	David Bentley	44	An OBE
20	False	45	Three
21	Southampton	46	1996
22	False	47	False
23	First	48	No
24	Monaco	49	Four
25	Reading	50	False

Crossword

ACROSS

1	Theo Walcott	14	Egypt
7	Ace	16	Solve
8	Leg	17	Feb
9	Tie	19	Ice
10	Swiss	20	Dog
12	Light	21	Eighty-eight

Wordsearch

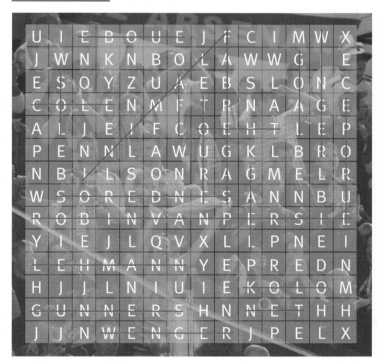

DOWN

1	Transfer fee	11	Icy
2	Eye	13	Gol
3	Wales	15	Twist
4	Legal	16	Steve
5	Out	18	Big
6	Twenty-eight	20	Dig

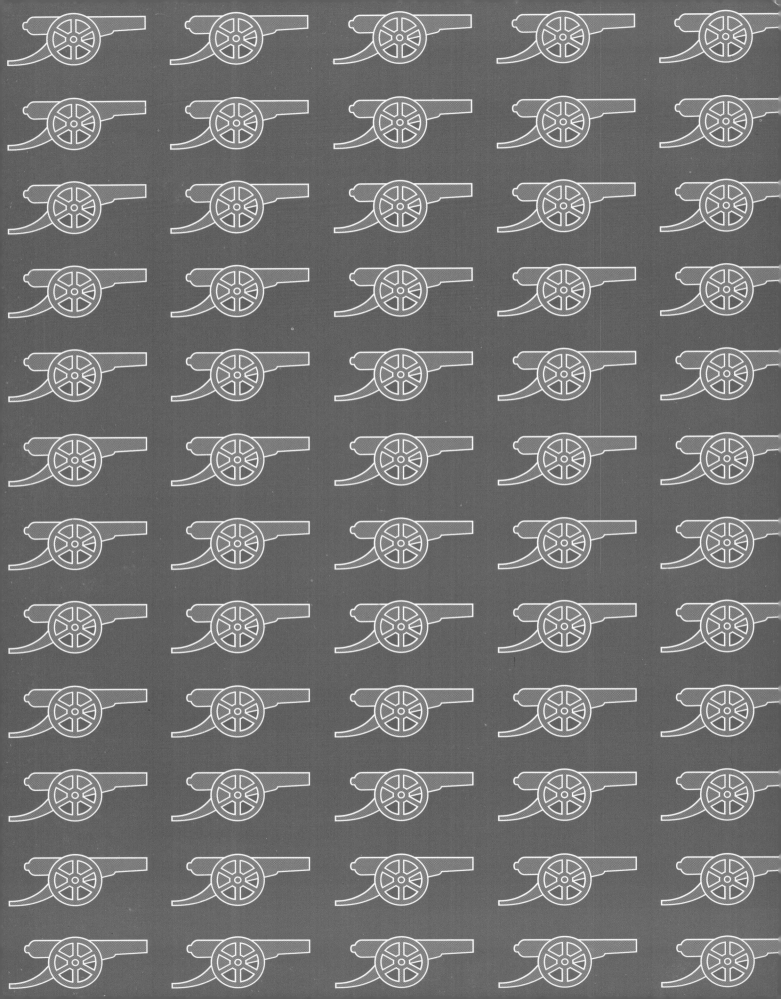